# What Happens
# When I Die?

# What Happens
## When I Die?

**TRUE STORIES** of the afterlife
and what they tell us about
**ETERNITY**

# BILL WIESE

**CHARISMA
HOUSE**

Most Charisma House Book Group products are available at special quantity discounts for bulk purchase for sales promotions, premiums, fund-raising, and educational needs. For details, write Charisma House Book Group, 600 Rinehart Road, Lake Mary, Florida 32746, or telephone (407) 333-0600.

What Happens When I Die? by Bill Wiese
Published by Charisma House
Charisma Media/Charisma House Book Group
600 Rinehart Road
Lake Mary, Florida 32746
www.charismahouse.com

Unless otherwise noted, all Scripture quotations are from the King James Version of the Bible.

Scripture quotations marked AMP are from the Amplified Bible. Old Testament copyright © 1965, 1987 by the Zondervan Corporation. The Amplified New Testament copyright © 1954, 1958, 1987 by the Lockman Foundation. Used by permission.

Scripture quotations marked NIV are from the Holy Bible, New International Version. Copyright © 1973, 1978, 1984, International Bible Society. Used by permission.

Scripture quotations marked NKJV are from the New King James Version of the Bible. Copyright © 1979, 1980, 1982 by Thomas Nelson, Inc., publishers. Used by permission.

Scripture quotations marked NLT are from the Holy Bible, New Living Translation, copyright © 1996, 2004, 2007. Used by permission of Tyndale House Publishers, Inc., Wheaton, IL 60189. All rights reserved.

Scripture quotations marked TLB are from The Living Bible. Copyright © 1971. Used by permission of Tyndale House Publishers, Inc., Wheaton, IL 60189. All rights reserved.

Cover design by Bill Johnson

Visit the author's website at www.soulchoiceministries.com.

Library of Congress Cataloging-in-Publication Data:
An application to register this book for cataloging has been submitted to the Library of Congress.
International Standard Book Number: 978-1-62136-276-0
E-book ISBN: 978-1-62136-277-7

While the author has made every effort to provide accurate telephone numbers and Internet addresses at the time of publication, neither the publisher nor the author assumes any responsibility for errors or for changes that occur after publication.

13 14 15 16 17 — 9 8 7 6 5 4 3 2
Printed in the United States of America

*I dedicate this book to my loving mother, who has prayed so faithfully for my wife and me. She has been the perfect example of what a Christian should be and has continually displayed a godly attitude in all situations. I am proud to be her son. I am also proud of my father. My parents have raised me and taught me integrity, honor, and the need to keep my word at all times. If there ever was a saint, my mother is one for certain. Mom and Dad, I love you both very much. Thank you for all you have done. May the Lord continue to bless you both, and may you live many more healthy years on this earth.*

With all our love,

Bill and Annette

# Contents

Acknowledgment . . . . . . . . . . . . . . . . . . . . . . . . . . . . . . . . xi

Introduction . . . . . . . . . . . . . . . . . . . . . . . . . . . . . . . . . . . xiii

Chapter 1: Gone in Three Seconds! . . . . . . . . . . . . . . . . . . 1

Chapter 2: Why Should I Go to Heaven? . . . . . . . . . . . . . . 7

Chapter 3: What Is Truth? . . . . . . . . . . . . . . . . . . . . . . . .20

Chapter 4: Informed or Ignorant? . . . . . . . . . . . . . . . . . . .30

Chapter 5: Near-Death Experiences . . . . . . . . . . . . . . . . . 43

Chapter 6: Clinical Death Experiences. . . . . . . . . . . . . . . 57

Chapter 7: Dreams and Visions of the Afterlife . . . . . . . .70

Chapter 8: Do You Believe in an Afterlife? . . . . . . . . . . . 83

Chapter 9: God Doesn't Give Up! . . . . . . . . . . . . . . . . . . .93

Chapter 10: The "Dead" Could Tell Us a
Thing or Two! . . . . . . . . . . . . . . . . . . . . . . . . . . . . .108

Chapter 11: What Religions Tell Us . . . . . . . . . . . . . . . . .115

Chapter 12: Why Is Christianity Unique? . . . . . . . . . . . . 131

Chapter 13: What Does the Bible Say About Hell? . . . . .142

Chapter 14: Have You Invested in Heaven? . . . . . . . . . . .158

Chapter 15: Losing Life to Find It! . . . . . . . . . . . . . . . . . .166

Chapter 16: Is It Really My Own Words? . . . . . . . . . . . . . 171

Chapter 17: Baptism—Is It a Requirement? . . . . . . . . . . 175

Appendix A:
Scriptures of Prophecy About Jesus
and Their Fulfillment. . . . . . . . . . . . . . . . . . . . . . . .180

Appendix B:
Comments on the Authenticity
of the Scriptures . . . . . . . . . . . . . . . . . . . . . . . . . . .184

Notes. . . . . . . . . . . . . . . . . . . . . . . . . . . . . . . . . . . . . . . . .191

# Acknowledgments

I WANT TO EARNESTLY thank my wonderful wife, Annette, who has stood faithfully by my side without waver and has worked so diligently in this ministry. She is exemplary as a Christian, as a helpmate, and utmost, as a loving wife. There would be no ministry, no books, and no public speaking if it wasn't for her. I am, of course, most thankful to the Lord for all He has done in my life and for giving me such a beautiful and exceptional wife. We travel everywhere together, and I would not have it any other way. Thank you, Annette, for all you are doing and for being the godly woman you are. I will love you always and forever.

—BILL

# Introduction

SINCE WE ARE all going to face death one day, why is there so little discussion in regard to where we will go after it happens? Why are there so many who remain unaware of what the Bible teaches about how one gains entrance into heaven? Are you aware of what other religions teach about heaven and hell? Are you aware of how the Bible differs in comparison to other religions? Have you ever read about the many legitimate experiences of those who claim to have seen heaven or hell? Can we take anything with us to heaven? Can we invest in our eternal life, just as we do in this present life? Since lying and deceit are so prevalent today, is it possible to know what real truth is? These are questions most of us would like answers to, and hopefully the small amount of knowledge I have gained over my forty-three years of study will shed some light on these questions. It would be wise of us to know what lies ahead after we die, before it is too late to change the outcome.

King Solomon said, "A prudent man foreseeth the evil, and hideth himself; but the simple pass on, and are punished" (Prov. 27:12).

The question is: Will you be the simple one, or will you be the wise one?

# 1

## Gone in Three Seconds!

W E LEFT THE house at 5:00 a.m. on April 18, 2012, on our way to the Los Angeles airport. We were heading to Charlotte, North Carolina, for a TV show. By 5:30 a.m. we were driving on the 405 freeway. We were in the inside lane of six lanes of heavy morning traffic, and all of a sudden, I felt like I was going to faint. I said to Annette, "Honey, I don't feel right. I think I am going to faint." And a second later I was passed out at the wheel—the car going sixty-five miles per hour. Now I have fainted several times in my lifetime, but this was different. There was not the normal wooziness or things starting to go dark before it happened. It was like there was an instant drop of power in my body, and then it was lights out. My wife had to maneuver the car across five other lanes of traffic. She had to get her leg over the console and situate her foot on the brake—and do all of this in the dark, as it was not light out yet. This was a miracle in itself—you know this if you have ever seen Los Angeles traffic! Thankfully we made it to the side of the freeway, and a couple of minutes later I regained consciousness—for about thirty seconds. My wife called emergency services. She knew something was not right, as I had never been ill or had any medical problems whatsoever before this. I have always been blessed with good health throughout my entire life. I had recently had an extensive physical and was found to be in excellent health. So what was the cause of my fainting spell?

Well, we had gone to a nutritionist to get some vitamins two days before this. The nutritionist recommended we take a certain vitamin that was good for circulation, since we sit on an airplane so often. It turns out that the so-called vitamin we were given was 85 percent nitric oxide. It is usually given to people with high blood pressure in order to lower it, as it opens up the veins and arteries. However, I already have a slow pulse rate and low blood pressure, so this "vitamin" inadvertently dropped my blood pressure down to almost nothing.

The ambulance arrived very quickly. The medics checked my pulse and said my heart was beating at only three beats per minute. They called out, "Precardiac!" and gave me an injection to raise my blood pressure, but that got my heartbeat up to only thirty beats per minute. Although my memory was fine, I couldn't get up and function properly. I felt dizzy, weak, and just terrible. The ambulance delivered me to the emergency room of the nearest hospital, and we ended up spending thirty-six miserable hours there while they ran every test known to man to be certain it wasn't something other than the pill I had taken.

Now my wife had taken the same pill at the same time as I did. She told me that as soon as I told her that I didn't feel right, she also felt a wave sweep over her body. It didn't cause her to pass out, as her blood pressure is normal, but it must have lowered hers a bit as well.

The hospital had to flush out the nitric oxide from my system with intravenous fluids for those thirty-six hours, and once it was out of my body, I felt fine and back to normal. All the test results revealed I was still in excellent condition. Thank God for that! But still, it was a terrifying experience, and it ended up costing us a lot of money and aggravation. This was because of one wrong decision to take one wrong pill. We usually read up on any vitamin we take, but we were in a hurry that morning. The doctor at the hospital told us that a nutritionist should never recommend that pill without taking a person's blood pressure first. He said that it could have caused permanent blindness or even killed me. The nutritionist had told us to take two pills. However, my wife felt a hesitation to take it and then suggested we take only one instead. She was hearing a warning from God, but she only acted on it partially. I'm so glad she picked up that much from the Lord or I would have most certainly been dead. Thank God for a godly wife! We could also easily have been killed on the freeway. Thank God for His protection.

Now I want to share what happened to me when I was passed out during that minute when I was lying on the side of the freeway. This is actually the relevant part of the story.

When I was unconscious, I saw myself sitting in a room and watching a video, but it wasn't a video for the purpose of entertainment. It was my entire life passing by at an incredibly high speed. I watched my whole life of sixty years in a single minute, and I could absorb it all. As the film approached the end, and as I was coming up on my current age, it began to slow up just a bit. When I regained consciousness, I found myself lying on the ground on the side of the freeway. The paramedics had pulled me out of the car. I didn't realize for a moment where I was or even what age I was. Traveling through the years of my life and then so abruptly ending that experience leaves you a bit disoriented. It was as if I had been placed back into life in order to complete the video.

When I found out I had almost died, I became aware of just how fragile life really is—and how quickly it can end. We are all going to die, but we really don't think it will happen to us. After my near-death experience I became keenly aware that there truly is an afterlife, and everything we do is all recorded—every second and every word we speak. I think today we can all relate to things being recorded, as we have e-mails, text messages, and telephone recorders. But God has a system that captures even the thoughts and intents of the heart. That is a pretty sophisticated system. It has caused me to be ever so conscious of my life in every area. What about you? Are you also paying attention to your actions, thoughts, and motives? The Bible states that we will all give an account of every word, thought, and action. (See Proverbs 12:14; Ecclesiastes 11:9; 12:14; Matthew 12:36; 16:27; Luke 12:3; 1 Corinthians 4:5; 6:9–10; Galatians 5:19–21; Ephesians 5:5; Revelation 21:8.) I wouldn't want my entire life shown to anyone. Yet, if we do not know Jesus, what we have spoken in darkness will be proclaimed from the housetops, and He will bring to light the hidden things of the heart. However, the Bible states that when we accept Jesus as our Lord and Savior and ask forgiveness of our sins, then God erases all our sins and remembers them no more. (See Psalm 103:11–12; Hebrews 8:12; 10:17). I am so grateful that all of the foolish things I have done are forgotten. Can you say the same? One more point: just as I made one wrong decision to take that pill, which almost cost me my life, we don't want to make one wrong decision in regard to where we will go for our eternal home!

There are many similar experiences others have had in seeing their lives play before their eyes. I will share one brief story written about in Dr. Maurice Rawlings's book, one reported by a Dr. Phillip Swihart. He documents the words of a patient at a hospital awaiting surgery:

> Next, blackness…Then it was light. I awoke and knew it was real. In front of me, I watched my whole life pass by. Every thought, word and every

movement I had made in my life....Every detail, right up to the present time. It all took place in what seemed to be a fraction of a second, and yet it was all very vivid.[1]

There have been thousands of stories chronicled in the numerous books about near-death experiences, those who were actually clinically dead, and those who have had dreams or visions of heaven and hell. I will be sharing some of these experiences, which I have read about or personally heard. I am not endorsing anyone. However, these stories I share seem to be credible. Hundreds have written to us during the past seven years sharing their experiences of death or their visions of heaven or hell. In almost every case each person had a total change of direction in life afterward, as it shook them to the core. They made a decision to follow Jesus and share the Word of God with others. Some entered the ministry, went to Bible college, or dedicated their lives to sharing God's Word. Most didn't want to share their experiences with anyone so as to avoid ridicule. But the thing that has also been consistent with most of their testimonies is what they reported seeing. In the visions of hell there were similar things, such as fire, tormented souls, demons of hatred, prison cells, loud cries, and the stench of burning sulfur. Those who saw heaven also saw similar things, such as people praising God, relatives who had preceded them in death, beautiful trees and grass, magnificent structures, streets of gold, gates of pearl, angels, and even Jesus Himself.

I am not attempting to duplicate what has already been done by many others, including some medical doctors. I am merely summarizing information that I have learned in order for you to be able to make an informed decision in regard to your own afterlife.

If we attend a funeral or visit a loved one in the graveyard, we must realize that most of the people who were laid to rest didn't expect to die when they did. We all somehow think that death won't happen to us. But one day it shows up at our door. All those people walked the earth just like us. They had their goals, their plans, and their families, and in a single moment of time, it was all over. As Randy Alcorn points out, "Worldwide, 3 people die every second, 180 every minute, and nearly 11,000 every hour…more than 250,000 people every day."[2]

The question is, where are they now? King David said, "LORD, make me to know mine end, and the measure of my days, what it is: that I may know how frail I am. Behold, thou hast made my days as a handbreadth; and mine age is as nothing before thee" (Ps. 39:4–5).

Proverbs 14:12 states: "There is a way which seemeth right unto a man, but the end thereof are the ways of death." The question we should all be asking ourselves is, am I certain where I will go after I die?

# 2

# Why Should I Go to Heaven?

I T IS USUALLY stated at funerals that the deceased person "has gone to a better place." And that is the case for many. But is that the case for all? Why do we assume that heaven is automatically achieved by everyone? The reason is, many of us think that we are good people, so we usually expect to end up there. But if entrance to heaven is based on being good, then whose standard of good should we go by? Yours and mine may differ.

Well, God's standard certainly differs from ours. His standard is this: if we lie once, steal one thing, have one lustful thought, or even have one foolish thought, it would exclude us from heaven. (See Proverbs 24:9; Ecclesiastes 12:14; Matthew 5:28; 12:36; 1 Corinthians 6:9; Galatians 5:19–21; Ephesians 5:5; Revelation 21:8.) That's a pretty high standard. James 2:10 states: "For whosoever shall keep the whole law, and yet offend in one point, he is guilty of all." If we break just one of His laws, we cannot be allowed into heaven. So that leaves all of us out. "Being good" is not our ticket into heaven. As a matter of fact Job 15:16 states, "How much more abominable and filthy is man, which drinketh iniquity like water?" Isaiah 64:6 states: "All our righteousnesses are as filthy rags; and we all do fade as a leaf; and our iniquities, like the wind, have taken us away." We cannot be allowed into heaven in our current fallen state. We are not as good as we think! It is like the young girl who was looking at the beautiful white sheep on the green hills. They appeared to be so pure white. Yet during the night it snowed and in the morning the hill was white with snow. She looked at the sheep, and suddenly they appeared to be dingy and dull. Compared to the pure white snow, the sheep looked dirty and gray. Well, we will look far worse when we are compared to a holy God! Thank God that our righteousness is not based on being good but on a relationship with Jesus Christ.

When God told Adam not to partake of the tree of the knowledge of good and evil (Gen. 2:17), He told him this because He did not want him to be separated from Him. He told him that he would die, not just physically but also spiritually. Spiritual death means to be cut off from God and all of life forever. It doesn't mean to "cease to exist." God also didn't want man to have any knowledge of evil. Once man understood evil, he would be tempted by it. However, man still sinned, even without the knowledge of evil, by disobeying God. God had withheld the knowledge of evil, so man didn't even know what evil was. God gave a command, which allowed man to have a free will to choose. God wanted man to have the choice to obey Him, thereby showing trust in His Word. His desire is for us to have a relationship with Him and obey Him out of love for Him. But Adam's sin separated us from God for all eternity.

Billy Graham states, "Death was the penalty for sin, and Adam and Eve made the choice of their own free wills. He told the first man and woman if they ate from the fruit of the tree of the knowledge of good and evil, they would die. But Satan scoffed at God's warning and told them they surely would not die. Adam and Eve chose to ignore God's warning and to believe Satan's lie."[1]

Now it was too late. Man had separated himself from God, as God told him he would. God could not simply annihilate man because He made us in His image (Gen. 1:26). We will live forever either with God or apart from Him. God now had to institute the plan He already had in order to redeem man back to Himself (Acts 2:23; 1 Cor. 2:7; 1 Pet. 1:20; Rev. 13:8.) God, of course, knew man would disobey Him.

Heaven and God are perfect, so He cannot let us into heaven the way we are because we would corrupt it, just as we have the earth (Isa. 24:5–6; 33:9; Rev. 21:27). We have to be given a new heart and a new spirit (Eccles. 11:19; Ezek. 11:19; 18:31; 36:26; 2 Cor. 5:17; Gal. 6:15), and that only comes through a relationship with Jesus Christ (John 3:3, 36).

Randy Alcorn says, "Because we are sinners, we are not entitled to enter God's presence. We cannot enter Heaven as we are. So Heaven is *not* our default destination. No one goes there automatically. Unless our sin problem is resolved, the only place we will go is our true default destination…Hell…Picture a single breath escaping your mouth on a cold day and dissipating into the air. Such is the brevity of life here. The wise will consider what awaits us on the other side of this life that so quickly ends."[2]

The second reason that being a good person doesn't get us into heaven is this: Suppose you found the most expensive home in the country, knocked on the door, and said, "Excuse me, but I'm moving into your home because I'm a good person!" What do you think the people would say? "No, of course not," right? You wouldn't expect them to allow that, as you don't know them. You have no relationship with them. Well, it is the same way with God. People go through their entire lives, they have nothing to do with God, they deny that Jesus is the Son of God, and they refuse to repent, which He said was the only way to enter His house, but then at the end of their lives they have the nerve to say to Him, "Excuse me, but I'm moving in with You, because I'm a good person!" What does "good" have to do with it? You don't even know Him! They expect to move into His house, and they even have the audacity to accuse Him of being mean if He doesn't let them in. They have no relationship with Him. He offered to be their Father throughout their entire lives, but they rejected Him and pushed Him away. You see, God is our Creator, but He is not our Father until we invite Jesus into our hearts as our Lord and Savior. At that point He becomes our Father. (See John 1:12; 8:44; 17:9; Romans 9:7–8; Galatians 3:26; Ephesians 1:5; 5:1.) Then we have the privilege of living in His house. So we would be the inconsiderate and arrogant ones to expect to live at someone's home whom we didn't know!

Another analogy might also help us see why *our* "good" falls short of *God's* idea of "good."

There were two men standing on a beach. One was very sickly and scrawny. He was asked to jump as far as he could, and he could only jump one foot. The other man was a picture of health, a gold-medal Olympian runner. He was asked to jump, and he hurled himself thirty-five feet through the air. A remarkable feat! Now they are both told that the goal is to jump from the shoreline in California to Hawaii. Well, it doesn't matter that the one is in such good shape. They will both need a boat. That's how far off we are when we say we are "good" enough to get into heaven. We all need the boat—and Jesus is that boat!

However, if you still want God to judge you on your good works, He will give you that opportunity. He will play back your entire life, your every action, your every thought, and your every motive at Judgment Day. (See Proverbs 12:14; 24:9; Ecclesiastes 11:9; Matthew 12:36; Luke 12:3; 1 Corinthians 4:5; 6:9–10; Galatians 5:19–21; Ephesians 5:5; Revelation 21:8.)

So do you really think you would look all that good if your entire life was shown before a holy God? I know I wouldn't. If we are honest, we're not all that good, even by our own mediocre standards. Thank God our salvation is not based on our good works. Please understand that good works should always follow after our acceptance of Him as our Lord and Savior. They should be evident in our lives, but good works don't get us saved. Good works are not the criteria for salvation; they are the result of salvation (Matt. 12:50; Luke 8:21; Heb. 5:9; 1 John 2:3, 17).

Since we live in a world that is filled with sin (1 John 5:19), we can become immune to its effects. We tolerate it every day. People lie to us or they try to cheat us. They usually are looking out for themselves. Since we are surrounded by sin every day, we tend to think that God is like that too, in that He will also tolerate it. We might think, "Why can not God simply overlook my sins? After all, my sin is minor and really not all that bad!" You might also wonder, "Why is sin so offensive to God? Why does our sin deserve an eternity of punishment? The punishment doesn't seem to fit the crime!"

First, let us look at why God cannot overlook our sin. We need to grasp the fact that sin cannot go unpunished. If God is going to be fair, then someone who commits a sin should not be let off scot-free. True justice always demands judgment, and God is a just God (Deut. 32:4; Ps. 96:10, 13; Isa. 45:21; Rom. 1:18; 2 Pet. 2:9). A good judge in our land would not be considered "good" if he let the criminal go free, right? How would you feel if your son or daughter was killed, and the judge simply let the killer go free? Well, our sin has to be paid for (Rom. 6:23), just as the criminal would need to pay for a murder. There are consequences for our actions. Since our sin is worthy of death, then God must exercise true justice. Now, if God were only a just God, we would all be sentenced to hell, with no possibility of being redeemed. However, since God is also love (1 John 4:16), He didn't leave man in that predicament. He provided a way of escape from the judgment on sin (1 Thess. 1:10). God decided to place all the punishment we deserve on His own Son, because of His great mercy and love for us. Jesus paid for our sins. If we reject Him, then we are left with our sins (John 8:24), and if we die in our sins, we cannot be allowed into heaven (Rev. 21:27).

Because of the seriousness of sin, the only way sin can be paid for is by the shedding of blood. Sin could only be paid for by the One who created man, Jesus Christ. He would need to become a man; live a perfect, sinless life; and then shed His blood for our sins (1 John 3:5). The Bible explains, "The life of the flesh is in the blood" (Lev. 17:11). Hebrews 9:22 states: "...and without shedding of blood is no remission." Since our sin is deserving of eternal punishment, it would also have to be shed by an eternal God. Only an eternal God could pay for our eternal sin. The punishment for our sin was severe, because sin is extremely offensive to a holy God. God couldn't let Jesus off easy and make His death as painless as possible, because our sin merited severe punishment. God didn't show Jesus favoritism just because He was His Son. The fact that God is 100 percent just means that He couldn't lighten up on the punishment on Jesus. Jesus endured the full wrath for us, and that also shows us He is 100 percent love. He is not 50 percent of each. He is 100 percent just and 100 percent love.

Another reason God cannot simply overlook our sin is this: God's very nature is different from ours. His nature is fire. Hebrews 12:29 states that "our God is a consuming fire." Nahum 1:5 also says, "The mountains quake at him, and the hills melt, and the earth is burned at his presence, yea, the world, and all that dwell therein." The entire world and all that is in it would be burned up at His presence because of His holy nature.

This analogy might help. Charles Stanley said, "Take fire, for example. Fire is hot by nature. Fire doesn't make itself hot; it *is* hot. That is the nature of fire. If you stuck your hand in a campfire to retrieve a hot dog that fell off your stick, you would be burned. You wouldn't get mad at the fire. You wouldn't say, 'I can't believe that fire burned me. I never did anything to the fire! Why would it treat me like that?' Fire and your hand are incompatible. They don't do well together."[3]

Since the nature of fire is to burn, and because the nature of God is to consume sin, then man being sinful becomes a problem. God's nature and our nature are also incompatible. It is not a matter of our sins being minor, and thereby being overlooked. It is because "any sin," even minor, cannot exist in His presence.

Billy Graham gives this simple illustration to show us how even a little sin corrupts and would defile heaven. He states: "Suppose you had a barrel of water and it had been filtered and distilled until no impurities remained. If someone asked you to drink it, you wouldn't hesitate. But suppose someone put a drop of raw sewage in it. Would you drink it? Of course not. The same is true with sin."[4]

I think we get the picture! Revelation 21:27 states: "And there shall in no wise enter into it [heaven] any thing that defileth."

Now, as to the next point, some try to reason that our seventy or eighty years of sin on this earth don't deserve an eternity of punishment. Again, they think, the punishment doesn't seem to fit the crime. Why is our sin so offensive to God? This next explanation will hopefully give us a clearer understanding as to why. Since we are sinning against a holy and infinitely powerful supreme being, it *is* truly deserving of eternal punishment.

Robert A. Peterson quotes Thomas Aquinas: "Now a sin that is against God is infinite; the higher the person against whom it is committed, the graver the sin. It is more criminal to strike a head of state than a private citizen—and God is of infinite greatness. Therefore an infinite punishment is deserved for a sin committed against him."[5]

To further explain, Christopher W. Morgan states: "If an angry teenage boy punched his mother, he would deserve more punishment than if he punched his older brother. The relationship and the offended party do matter. It is also important to remember that God is not only different from human beings in degree; he is also different in being. If in a robbery, the gunman shoots and kills the owner of the house, he should receive a greater punishment than if he killed the family cat (as much as this writer loves cats!). Thus, because sin is against God, and God is infinitely worthy of obedience, sin merits an infinite punishment."[6]

So the greater the one sinned against, the graver the sin. And again, if I lie to you it would be wrong, but if I lie to the Supreme Court, it would be worse, because of their position. If I step on a bug and kill it, it would be no big deal, even though it is the taking of a life. If I kill a dog or a cat, it would be much worse. Yet if I kill a human being, it would be much, much worse. Killing a human being deserves a greater punishment than killing a cat! Why? It is because of the greater essence of the "being." Well, God is infinitely greater in "position" and in "being," and therefore sin against Him is deserving of eternal punishment. It took an eternal God to die for our eternal sin. Romans 7:13 says, "…that sin by the commandment might become exceeding sinful." Sin is exceedingly evil to God.

As Dr. Chuck Missler points out, "We don't understand the magnitude of sin on the one hand; we can't appreciate the majesty of God on the other. Part of the seriousness of sin isn't just the intrinsic part of sin itself, but it's who it is against. And when it is against an infinite being, sin is against the character of an infinite being."[7]

In addition to why our sin is deserving of eternal

punishment, there are also these two points. First, if we spent say, two hundred years in hell or a certain amount of time in payment for our sins, then that would be considered "works." After the time was up, we would be saying to God, "I paid for my sins. It's time to let me out." However, the Bible says we are saved by grace, not by works (Eph. 2:8–9). Time is the wrong premise and could never suffice. Time cannot pay for sins; only the shed blood of an eternal God could pay for sins (Rom. 5:9; Heb. 9:22; 1 John 1:7).

The second point is this. God sent His most precious Son to die for us. Many people reject what God values most. They are, in essence, saying to God, "I do not value Your Son. He means nothing to me, so don't bother me with Your views. I have my own." As a matter of fact, people even use His Son's name as a curse word throughout their entire lives. How would you feel if you gave up your own son to die for someone, and they blasphemed his name and even denied that he existed? Hebrews 10:29 states, "Of how much worse punishment, do you suppose, will he be thought worthy who has trampled the Son of God underfoot?" (NKJV). It goes on to say, "It is a fearful thing to fall into the hands of the living God" (v. 31).

God hates all sin, and there are also varying degrees of sin. Jesus said to Pilate in John 19:11, "He that delivered me unto thee hath the greater sin." In Matthew 23:14 Jesus mentions that the hypocrites "shall receive the greater damnation." In Proverbs 6:16–17 the Lord lists six things He hates: "Yea, seven are an abomination unto him." But any sin will exclude us from heaven.

Yet, even though God hates all sin, He is a God of great mercy and grace. He gives many warnings and time for us to change our ways. He shows man His goodness, His patience, His kindness, and His forgiveness. Psalm 86:5 states, "For thou, LORD, art good, and ready to forgive; and plenteous in mercy unto all them that call upon thee." Psalm 145:8–9 states: "The LORD is gracious, and full of compassion; slow to anger, and of great mercy. The LORD is good to all: and his tender mercies are over all his works." (See also Luke 6:35; Romans 15:5; Revelation 1:9.) His desire is to see everyone repent and receive Him as their Lord and Savior and enter heaven (John 5:40; 6:40; 11:25–26; Acts 2:21; Rom. 10:13; Eph. 2:8–9; 1 Tim. 2:4–6; 2 Pet. 3:9). He will never force anyone to believe in Him. Actually, the only time Jesus ever used force was when He threw people *out* of the temple (Matt. 21:12; Mark 11:15; Luke 19:45; John 2:14–15). He never forced anyone in!

Dr. Robert A. Peterson points out John 3:16–18, which explains the purpose of Jesus's coming. He states: "God did not send his Son into the world to condemn the lost, but to rescue them from hell (v. 17). Here we learn of God's heart; he loves sinners and commissions his Son as a missionary to reach them. Jesus comes to them in love, offering salvation freely to all who will receive it. Believers in Christ need not wait for the Judgment Day to learn God's verdict (v. 18). The Judge has come before that day as the Savior. In this capacity he announces the rulings of the Last Day ahead of time. All who trust Jesus as Savior, therefore, have already received God's verdict of no condemnation. Unbelievers, however, receive the opposite verdict—that of condemnation (v. 18). They too need not wait for the Last Day; based upon their rejection of God's Son they can know now that they are heading for hell. Oh that they would heed God's warning, turn from their sins, and accept Jesus' gift of salvation. The Son of God did not come into the world to condemn sinners any more than missionaries go into other cultures to condemn people. In both cases the motivation for going is love!"[8]

So I ask you: Why should any of us go to heaven? Do you

feel entitled to be admitted to this perfect place? Many today feel entitled to almost everything. We want the expensive car early in life. We want the nice home and the job paying the big bucks right away, without earning our advancement. This mentality pervades our culture and carries over into spiritual matters, as well. We expect heaven—as if we deserve it. The truth is, no one deserves it!

Billy Graham says, "Why do some people believe they have a paid ticket to heaven? They give many answers. The first is, 'Just look at what I've done on earth. My record is pretty good, compared to some. I'll be in heaven because I lived such a good life.' That person is in trouble. The Bible says, 'For all have sinned and fall short of the glory of God' (Romans 3:23)....No one can ever live a life that is 'good enough'. The Bible says, 'For whoever keeps the whole law and yet stumbles at just one point is guilty of breaking all of it' (James 2:10). The second answer might be, 'I really don't know, and I'm not sure that I care. I gave it some thought for a while, but there were so many other things that seemed more important.'"9

## Is There Only One Way?

Some people think Christians are narrow-minded to think there is only one way to heaven. Some go as far as to consider these beliefs a hate crime. They somehow twist the truth of "being specific" with "being prejudiced."

If we have a disease and go to a doctor, and he or she explains that "there is only one known cure, and here is the pill for that cure. It will rid you of the disease," we wouldn't say to the doctor, "I'm offended! There must be more than one cure, and I am not going to accept this pill." No, of course not! We would be grateful for the cure and gladly take the medicine. In the same way, all of humanity has a disease.

It is called "sin" (Rom. 3:23; 5:8, 13–14, 17–19). There is only one antidote, and it is Jesus Christ (John 10:28; Acts 4:12).

No one else paid for our sins (John 12:47; 1 Cor. 15:3–4; 1 Tim. 1:15; 2:4–6). No one else died in our place and rose from the dead. Just receive the antidote, and you will be cured (Luke 13:3; Rom. 10:9–10). Why do we argue? God gives specific directions to follow in order for us to get to His house. How can this be interpreted as prejudice?

We all are accustomed to following directions in life. We have our smart devices and our navigation systems. When we are given directions to someone's house, we follow them specifically. So why is it so difficult to follow God's directions to heaven?

Suppose you invited me over to dinner in your home, and you give me exact directions to follow. You tell me to "go south on highway 95, turn right at Main Street, and then proceed up the hill, and you will come to my house. That is the only way to get to my house." Then I say to you, "No, I think I will go north on 95, then turn left on MacArthur Boulevard, because I think all roads lead to your house." You would then explain to me, "You will not get to my house that way. I'm trying to give you clear directions. Just follow them." In the same way, God gives us clear directions to His house. I think God knows where He lives! All we have to do is follow His clear directions and we will get there. He is not being narrow-minded; He is being specific. He is trying to get us to His house, not keep us out.

We are accustomed to specifics. If an airplane is going to fly, it must be constructed with a very specific design. The wing must be configured a certain way in order to create lift. The engine must be of a certain thrust in order to create enough speed to cause the lift and thereby supersede the law of gravity. Most surgeries work correctly only one way. Most things in life work correctly only one way. So why do we completely abandon our everyday practices when it comes to spiritual matters? Many will say, "Whatever you believe is fine for you, and whatever I believe is also OK." Now this kind of rhetoric and loose thinking is due to a lack of knowledge. We pride ourselves on being able to discuss any subject and to be considered open-minded. Yet when it comes to biblical matters, many will not even discuss it. This is one reason why there is such widespread ignorance of the way to get to heaven.

# 3

# What Is Truth?

PILATE WAS TALKING with Jesus just before he was pressured into condemning Him to death. Jesus told him that His kingdom was not of this world. Pilate asked Him if He was a king. Jesus said He was, and He continued, "To this end was I born, and for this cause came I into the world, that I should bear witness unto the truth. Every one that is of the truth heareth my voice. Pilate saith unto him, What is truth? And when he had said this, he went out again unto the Jews, and saith unto them, I find in him no fault at all" (John 18:37–38). Pilate knew how elusive truth was, but he must have believed Jesus was, in fact, telling him the truth. His question about truth was cynical, yet he sensed that Jesus was honest and spoke the truth. It caused him to seek to free Him. The crowd, however, insisted on having Him crucified, which was what God had intended from the beginning.

We have become callous to knowing what "truth" is in life because of how commonplace it has become for people to lie or cover up the truth. If we are purchasing a home or a car, we are skeptical, as so many people do not disclose all the facts. Our politicians so often are not telling us the truth. Jesus said this in John 14:6: "I am the way, the truth, and the life: no man cometh unto the Father, but by me." He clearly declares that He is the truth. Some believe there is no God. They state that God cannot be proven to exist. However, there are many books written offering overwhelming proof that the entire Bible is true. I have listed some comments by the experts in regard to the validity of the Bible in Appendix B.

There is also something else to consider: if someone believes that there is no God, then there can be no explanation on why man has a conscience. Where would he have obtained it, since no animal has any such thing? Where did ethics and morals come from? Why does man have an understanding heart, since no animal does? God asked that question to Job: "…or who hath given understanding to the heart?" (Job 38:36). Man cannot answer that question apart from God!

William Lane Craig explains, "Consider, then, moral values. If theism is false, why think that human beings have objective moral value? After all, on the naturalistic view, there's nothing special about human beings. They're just accidental byproducts of nature which have evolved relatively recently on an infinitesimal speck of dust called the planet Earth, lost somewhere in a hostile and mindless universe, and which are doomed to perish individually and collectively in a relatively short time. Richard Dawkins' assessment of human worth may be depressing, but why, on atheism, is he mistaken when he says, 'There is at bottom no design, no purpose, no evil, no good, nothing but pointless indifference.…We are machines propagating DNA.'"[1]

Dr. Craig goes on to say: "…it is precisely humanists themselves who seek to find a special place for the human species in the scheme of things, who refuse to accept the full implications of reducing human beings to just another animal species. For humanists continue to treat human beings as *morally* special in contrast to other species. What justification is there for this differential treatment?…Crudely put, on the atheistic view human beings are just animals, and animals have no moral obligation to one another.…Why think that if God does not exist, we would have any moral obligations to do anything? Who or what imposes these moral duties upon us?"[2]

For the most part our society has set truth aside and declared that there are no absolutes. However, in not defining what is right or wrong and good or evil, we have set ourselves up to be held hostage to every fanatical belief that comes along. And if we don't embrace everyone's personal beliefs, we are considered intolerant.

Robert Jeffress states it this way: "Why has the quest for tolerance replaced the quest for truth as the highest ideal? Because of the unquestioned assumption that absolute truth leads to hatred and oppression. That assumption is already widely accepted today in the academic world. For example, several months after the terrorist attacks of September 11, 2001, former president Bill Clinton addressed the students at Georgetown University and partly blamed the attacks on America's 'arrogant self-righteousness.' If only both sides could realize that there is no such thing as absolute truth, perhaps this catastrophe could have been avoided, Clinton suggested. 'Nobody's got the truth.... We are incapable of ever having the whole truth.' ... This demonization of those who claim absolute truth has spilled over into the world of evangelical Christianity. One Gallup poll revealed that 88 percent of evangelical Christians believe that the 'Bible is the written word of God and is totally accurate in all it teaches.' Yet, of those same evangelicals, 53 percent claimed that there are no absolute truths! Why? They have accepted hook, line, and sinker the assumption that exclusivity promotes hatred."[3]

Charles Colson writes: "Art Lindsley...in his excellent book *True Truth: Defending Absolute Truth in a Relativistic World*...writes, 'Just as a need to relate truth to all areas of life does not make us relativists, so believing that there are some moral absolutes does not make us absolutists...' As Lindsley writes, 'Relativists consistently stand guilty of the philosophical sin of making exceptions to their own absolute rules.' They claim that Christianity is a religion of intolerance...that Christians shouldn't impose their values on others but leave them free to choose their own value systems. But where did they get their ideas of tolerance and justice—of right and wrong in general—if they genuinely don't believe in moral absolutes? Without such ideas, how can anyone formulate a meaningful system of values?"[4]

One writer said that a man doesn't call a line crooked unless he has some idea of a straight line. Carl F. H. Henry said, "The widespread questioning of authority is condoned and promoted in many academic circles. Philosophers with a radically secular outlook have affirmed that God and the supernatural are mythical conceptions...all beliefs and ideals are declared to be relative to the age and culture in which they appear.... The Bible's claim to divine authority is dismissed by such thinkers.... In the name of man's supposed 'coming of age,' radical secularism champions human autonomy and creative individuality. Man is his own lord and the inventor of his own ideals and values, it is said. He lives in a supposedly purposeless universe that has itself presumably been engendered by a cosmic accident. Therefore, human beings are declared to be wholly free to impose upon nature and history whatever moral criteria they prefer."[5]

Some will accuse the Christian of being judgmental and condemning. However, to "judge" is to find a person guilty and implies punishment. The word *judge* means "to pass judgment upon in a court of law...to pass sentence upon; condemn."[6]

Christians do not instill punishment by any means. A Christian merely informs someone of the way to *avoid* a future punishment, which will be brought by God not the

Christian. And God doesn't even want to punish the wrong-doer; He wants to forgive them!

This is simply a message of warning, which is a message of love. What loving parent wouldn't warn their child not to play in a busy street? God is giving us a warning, because He loves everyone and wants us to come and live in His house. He doesn't force anyone, and neither does the Christian. It is each person's own choice.

As Franklin Graham points out: "Jesus was wonderfully tolerant in the way He dealt with people as we see when He met the woman of Samaria. Jews during this time had little to do with the despised Samaritans. But Jesus did not participate in what would have been 'politically correct' racial or sexual prejudice. He was compassionate and tolerant toward the sinner but knew how to draw the line when it came to the sinfulness in a person's life.... Jesus spoke with compassion and understanding, and He explained to her spiritual truths so well that she left her water pot and went into the city and told the men what had happened and much of the city came to meet Jesus.... Jesus' followers assumed He would want to squelch those who did not agree with Him. But instead, Jesus was tolerant and dealt with those of other faiths in kindness and love."[7]

The bottom line is that many do not want to be told that there are truths and absolutes in life because it makes them accountable for their actions. There are consequences for our choices, but so many people believe that they are "good" people and therefore deserve whatever is good. They feel entitled to receive "good" things in life, and they expect the same in the afterlife—not realizing that "good" will not get anyone into heaven.

Charles Colson says, "We must ask people to face the stark choice: either a worldview that maintains that we are inherently good or a worldview that acknowledges a transcendent standard and our accountability before a holy God for our sin. The first choice eventually leads to moral anarchy and opens the door to tyranny; the second choice makes possible an ordered and morally responsible society. When Jewish theologian Dennis Prager gives speeches, he often asks audiences to imagine that they are walking down a dark city alley at night and they suddenly see a group of young men coming toward them. Prager then asks: 'Would you be frightened or relieved that they are carrying Bibles and that they've just come from a Bible study?' Audiences invariably laugh and admit that they would be relieved. Commitment to biblical truth leads to more civil behavior."[8]

As one writer pointed out that, truth is being privatized. In today's society whatever is truth to you should not be viewed as untruth by others. If a person or group stands up for a certain truth that opposes another's, it would be considered intolerance.

However, if truth is privatized, then we have approximately seven billion opinions of what truth is. Jesus said He is that "Truth." If we don't embrace this fact, our nation will crumble. The principles in the Bible teach us that all are created equal and that freedom is for all to enjoy. There are no prejudices in the Bible. In addition, Christianity does not force its beliefs on anyone. We are taught to respect everyone's beliefs and opinions, but not to tolerate anyone's evil agenda. We should not be afraid or intimidated to stand up for our convictions. The extremists push their evil agendas on others who sometime disagree with them but who don't voice their disagreement for fear of being thought of as intolerant. People treat tolerance these days as if it were a virtue. Tolerance should not be confused with consideration. We should be considerate of all but intolerant of evil. Jesus did not tolerate evil. He said, "But woe unto you, scribes, and Pharisees, hypocrites! for ye shut up the kingdom of heaven against men: for ye neither go in yourselves, neither suffer ye them that are entering to go in...for ye compass sea and land to make one proselyte, and when he is made, ye make him twofold more the child of hell than yourselves" (Matt. 23:13, 15). He condemned the scribes and Pharisees for causing people to go to hell, as they were doing.

In Revelation 2:2 Jesus commended the Church of Ephesus because, as He said, "I know you don't tolerate sin among your members..." (TLB). He commended them for not tolerating sin, but in Revelation 2:20 He condemned the church of Thyatira, saying, "You tolerate the woman Jezebel...who is teaching and leading astray my servants...into practicing sexual vice..." (AMP). Here Jesus is stating that it is wrong to tolerate sexual sin, and it is right to be intolerant of evil. This is just the opposite of what goes on in today's society.

John Adams said, "Suppose a Nation in some distant region should take the Bible for their only law book, and every member should regulate his conduct by the precepts there exhibited! Every member would be obligated in conscience to temperance, frugality, and industry; to justice, kindness, and charity towards his fellow men; and to piety, love, and reverence toward Almighty God....What a Utopia, what a Paradise would this region be."[9]

There was an article written by MSNBC in 2004. Its headline stated: "Belief in Hell Boosts Economic Growth, Fed Says." The article itself states, "Fear of the nether world is a disincentive to wrongdoing....Economists searching for reasons why some nations are richer than others have found that those with a wide belief in hell are less corrupt and more prosperous, according to a report by the Federal Reserve Bank of St. Louis....The St. Louis Fed drew on work by outside economists who studied 35 countries, including the United States, European nations, Japan, India and Turkey and found that religion sheds some useful light."[10]

The belief in even just one doctrine of the Bible causes a nation to be less corrupt: "Hold fast to the Bible as the sheet anchor of your liberties; write its principles upon your hearts, and practice them in your lives."[11]

There are those who say that society has changed and evolved into the realization that the Bible and its teachings are out of touch with our modern world. They state that we must grow with popular opinion and become more relative. However, I have learned that opinions change, but truth does not. One writer said, "The truth does not change according to our ability to stomach it."[12]

I remember that when I was young, if you asked most people what the capital of New York State was, they would answer, "New York City." But just because it was what many people believed doesn't make it right. There was a time when science thought the earth was flat. There was a time, up until 1845, when hand washing for a surgeon at a hospital was thought unnecessary. How absurd was that! There was a time when they thought the cell was simple. Grant R. Jeffrey writes, "In 1963, scientists finally penetrated the initial mysteries of the cellular wall.... George Palade, a professor of the Rockefeller Institute in New York...was amazed to discover an unbelievably intricate and complex system throughout the protoplasm."[13]

People change, opinions change, and morals change, but truth never changes. The Bible has established these truths, and without the Bible there would be no standard and authority for truth. Our laws are based on the Ten Commandments, so we do have absolutes established on God's Word. And these biblical principles are beneficial to all. However, as Christians we also need to have the correct attitude, as Jesus did, which will help in persuading any person to consider embracing biblical authority. It is with a humble attitude that we should approach those who oppose us, and not an attitude of condemnation. The demeanor of Christ is always the most effective defense of the truths of the Bible.

Rod Parsley states, "We don't embrace a biblical world-view so we can feel smug and superior in our correctness. We do it so we can get down where people are struggling and, from a position of strength, help them. We must possess a clear understanding of the ways in which people are deceived—not so we can condemn them, but so we can reason with them."[14]

So where are we headed? Attorney Charles Crismier sums it up nicely: "Truth lies trampled in the streets of a nation whose first president 'could not tell a lie.'...So life careens into an endless and tumultuous sea that has no absolutes suitable for anchor, and we have no compass with which to gain a clear perspective and no maps with which to chart our direction. We are plunging recklessly and almost frantically into uncharted waters, oblivious to where we are headed. Together, we have been cut loose on the sea of relativity, and we are in desperate need of a beacon from God's lighthouse—the truth from a God who does not change with every vacillation of human experience, a truth that can steer us clear of the looming shoals of personal and national destruction....Drift leads to decadence, as the following statistics testify.

"Ninety-one percent of us lie regularly, telling conscious, premeditated lies...

"Only 13 percent of us believe in all of the Ten Commandments. There is absolutely no moral consensus in the country.

"Thirty-three percent of all our children are born illegitimate.

"Eighty percent of our children in our larger cities are illegitimate."[15]

I could cite many more alarming statistics, and the trend continues as our nation becomes less and less godly. The straight line of truth has become blurred, and even erased in many cases. The Bible states it this way in Isaiah 5:20: "Woe unto them that call evil good, and good evil; that put darkness for light, and light for darkness." Psalm 94:20 says, "Shall the throne of iniquity have fellowship with thee, which frameth mischief by a law?" In other words, when the evil man wants to promote his mischievous agenda, he makes up a law in order to enforce his wickedness.

First Corinthians 13:6 says, "[Love] does not rejoice in iniquity, but rejoices in the truth" (NKJV).

Charles Colson states, "Christians must boldly cultivate a biblical worldview, dismantling the postmodern notion that truth is whatever 'feels right.'"[16]

Once someone individually or an entire society rejects the truth, they will embrace any foolish doctrine that comes along. Second Timothy 4:4 states, "And they shall turn away their ears from the truth, and shall be turned unto fables." Let us wake up and stand for righteousness, resist evil, get the Bible back into our schools, and save this great nation in which we live.

# 4

# Informed or Ignorant?

MARK TWAIN ONCE quipped, "We are all ignorant; just about different things."[1] Thomas Edison stated, "We do not know one-millionth of one percent about anything."[2] How often have we been convinced about a thing, and then later discovered we were in error? Even science has declared some things to be so-called facts, and as man gained more knowledge, he found out he was wrong. John D. Morris, PhD, states, "Today we can watch as the concept of evolution self-destructs. It has never been well supported by the evidence, and now many scientists are coming forward to point out its weaknesses. Many have recognized the total inability of chance, random processes to produce the incredible complexity we see around us—especially in living systems."[3]

In looking at the design of the universe—and all of creation—we should recognize that there obviously must be a designer (Rom. 1:19–21). To our awareness, our earth is the only planet with life on it, and every aspect of it has been finely tuned for our benefit. Look at the remarkable birth of a baby or the complexity of the human cell (Ps. 139:14). Lee Strobel quotes Walter L. Bradley, PhD, in regard to the so-called simple cell. He states, "…a one-cell organism is more complicated than anything we've been able to recreate through supercomputers."[4]

Look at the design of the human body, with its symmetrical

balance, its ability to heal itself, and its remarkable capabilities. Was this all caused by just a series of accidents? Look at the incredible design of the human eye. Grant R. Jeffrey quotes Charles Darwin, who "himself admitted... 'To suppose that the eye with all its inimitable contrivances for adjusting the focus to different distances, for admitting different amounts of light, and for the correction of spherical and chromatic aberration, could have formed by natural selection, seems, I freely confess, absurd in the highest degree.'"[5] Grant goes on to say, "We are generally impressed when highway engineers are able to correctly align two thirty-foot-wide tunnels dug from opposite sides of a mountain to meet precisely in the center of the mountain. However, every day, hundreds of thousands of children are born with the ability to see, their bodies having precisely aligned one million separate optic nerves from each eye to meet their matching optic-nerve endings growing out from the baby's brain. Anyone who believes this miracle of design happens by chance probably still believes in Santa Claus."[6]

Look at what insight the Bible mentions about the blood. Again, Grant Jeffrey goes on to say: "Thousands of years ago, Moses wrote these words in the Bible that reveal scientific and medical knowledge far in advance of its day: 'For the life of the flesh is in the blood' (Lev. 17:11). How could Moses have known three thousand years ago what doctors did not know until the discovery, by the English doctor Dr. William Harvey in 1616, of the essential role of the circulation of blood in the function of life."[7]

God told Abraham to circumcise newborn males on the eight day (Gen. 17:12). Why the eighth day? "On the eighth day, the amount of prothrombin present is actually elevated above one-hundred percent of normal—and is the only day in the male's life in which this will be the case under normal conditions. If surgery is to be performed, day eight is the

31

perfect day to do it. Vitamin K and prothrombin levels are at their peak."[8] "It appears (based on data) that on the eighth day after birth, an infant baby has more available prothrombin than any other day of his life, making the eighth day the best time for circumcision."[9]

Consider the vastness and the precision of the universe (Ps. 147:4; Isa. 40:12; 48:13). Observe the earth: What is turning it in such a precise and even manner? (See Genesis 8:22.) What if it varied just a fraction of a degree in angle or varied its speed of turning? Catastrophic storms would develop. How is it that the earth is simply hung on nothing (Job 26:7, 38:4; Ps. 104:5)? Science thought the earth was flat for many centuries. Yet God told us it was round eight hundred years before Christ was born (Isa. 40:22). What keeps the vast oceans from moving onto the land (Gen. 9:11; Job 38:11; Ps. 104:9; Prov. 8:29)? And here is another interesting point: man didn't know about the springs in the sea until approximately the 1970s, according to Steven A. Austin, PhD.[10] Yet God told us about them in Job 38:16, over three thousand years ago. There are also the river currents or paths that run through the seas. These were not fully discovered until the 1800s. Yet God told Isaiah and David about these paths three thousand years ago (Ps. 8:8; 77:19; Isa. 43:16). God also told Solomon about the wind having circuits (Eccles. 1:6), which science didn't understand until recently. Another thing God told Job was that light could be parted, as a laser does (Job 38:24). In addition, man thought until recently that darkness was simply the absence of light. Yet God says that darkness has a place (Job 38:19), like possibly a black hole in space. In addition, Job 37:9 states, "Out of the south cometh the whirlwind..." How could Job have known that a hurricane would originate in the south? In Job 36:27–28, God told Job about the rain: "Which the clouds do drop and distil upon man abundantly." How could Job have known about the water in the clouds being distilled? Most of the water vapor is from the oceans, which are full of salt, and if it wasn't distilled, it would kill plant life and man couldn't drink it. "In nature, the sun evaporates water into the air, where it rises and is captured by clouds. With the colder temperatures of the clouds, the evaporated water (steam) is condensed back into water and it falls back onto the earth as pure rain water."[11]

"A recent study by the United States Department of Agriculture proved that most of the water that forms into clouds worldwide comes from the evaporation of the waters found in the oceans."[12] In Genesis 6:14–16 God gave the dimensions of the ark to Noah to build. "In 1609 at Hoorn in Holland, a ship was built after that same pattern, and this revolutionized shipbuilding. By 1900 every large ship on the high seas was inclined toward the proportions of the ark (as verified by 'Lloyd's Register of Shipping' in the *World Almanac*)."[13] In Job 38:35 God asks Job, "Canst thou send lightnings, that they may go, and say unto thee, Here we are?" Lightning is electricity. Our voices are carried by electricity through the telephone, and at the other end of the line our voice is heard.

Look at the animal kingdom, plant life, and even the many species of fish. There is intricate and delicate design in every single form of life. There are birds that fly to certain islands to procreate. There are whales that travel great distances to reach a certain area each year. Who programmed them to know these things?

Look at the laws of gravity, magnetism, electricity, the balance of the ozone layers, and so forth. Scientists state that if any one of these things is off in even the slightest amount, life would cease to exist. Where did that delicate balance come from? What about all the variety of food that grows in order to sustain life—and it is even good to taste? Another coincidence, I suppose!

Look at the existence of the male and female genders in almost every species, designed in order to procreate. How did that happen just by chance? There are far too many of these convenient coincidences to believe everything happened by accident. Science tells us that in the beginning there was nothing, and then one day, nothing exploded! How scientific is that statement?

We know that the frog becoming a prince is a fairy tale. Yet science tells us that an ape, or even worse, a slimy amoeba, or even worse yet, nothing at all, one day exploded and became a man! The way scientists get us to buy this fairy tale is to simply say that it took millions of years. They add "time" to the ingredients and then people buy it. We think that somehow all this order will come into place over a long period of time. Yet time is actually an enemy to order and progression, if you study the facts. "The universe...is decaying...every system tends to become disordered.... And the second law (of Thermodynamics) says that disorder or randomness tends to increase."[14]

Evolutionists ignore this fundamental law of physics because it contradicts their theory. The Bible states that there is a Creator, and it is obvious there is intelligent design everywhere we look. To deny it, one is said by God to be a fool (Ps. 14:1; 53:1).

Professor Paul C. W. Davies puts it this way: "Alternatively the numerical coincidences could be regarded as evidence of design. The delicate fine-tuning in the values of the constants, necessary so that the various branches of physics can dovetail so felicitously, might be attributed to God. It is hard to resist the impression that the present structure of the Universe, apparently so sensitive to minor alterations in the numbers, has been rather carefully thought out."[15]

The astronomer Dr. Paul Davis said, "There is for me powerful evidence that there is something going on behind it all....It seems as though somebody has fine-tuned nature's numbers to make the Universe....The impression of design is overwhelming."[16]

Sir Fred Hoyle, a committed evolutionist, said, "A commonsense interpretation of the facts [concerning the energy levels in 12 Carbon and 16 Oxygen] suggests that a super-intellect has monkeyed with physics, as well as with chemistry and biology, and that there are no blind forces worth speaking about in nature."[17]

"Professor Robert Jastrow, although he is an agnostic, admits that, 'the Universe was constructed within very narrow limits, in such a way that man could dwell in it. This result is called the anthropic principle. It is the most theistic result ever to come out of science, in my view.'"[18]

Astronomer Alan Sandage wrote: "I find it quite improbable that such order came out of chaos. There has to be some organizing principle. God to me is a mystery but is the explanation for the miracle of existence, why there is something instead of nothing."[19]

Some state that all those in the Bible were ignorant or unlearned people. That is clearly not the case. Throughout history people have been relatively intelligent. There are also many successful and brilliant people mentioned in the Bible who believed in Jesus Christ as the Lord and Savior or, in the Old Testament, who looked forward to that Savior (Gen. 15:6; Ps. 49:15; 51:1–5; Isa. 25:8; 45:22; Hosea 13:4). Here are just a few:

> » Abraham had three hundred trained servants in his household (Gen. 13:6; 14:14). He was very rich in much cattle, silver, and gold (Gen. 13:2; 24:35). He had so much that he and Lot could not dwell together in the land. Abraham was called "the Friend of God" (2 Chron. 20:7; Isa.

41:8; James 2:23). He is the father of faith, as he was proven in the ultimate test of faith in God (Gen. 22:2, 9–12; Heb. 11:17). God chose him because God said in Genesis 18:19, "For I know him, that he will command his children and his household after him, and they shall keep the way of the LORD, to do justice and judgment." That doesn't sound like a foolish or unlearned man!

» Joseph was second in command in all of Egypt, appointed by Pharaoh himself. The pharaoh said there was none as wise as Joseph. He was also a very prosperous man, and the Lord is the one who prospered him (Gen. 39:2–5, 41:39–46; Acts 7:10).

» Moses was trained in all the knowledge of Egypt (Acts 7:22). He led over three million people out of Egypt. He was called God's friend (Exod. 33:11). Only two people were ever called God's friend in the Old Testament, and Moses was one of them. He judged all the people with wisdom, and they brought all the hard cases to him, after he placed others under him to help judge the people (Exod. 18:13–26). His name is mentioned 848 times in the Bible. Exodus 11:3 says that "Moses was very great in the land of Egypt." He is the only man to ever see God's back parts (Exod. 33:23), because "Thou canst not see my face: for there shall no man see me, and live" (v. 20). He is the only person in the Bible, except for Jesus, to have fasted for forty days without food or water, and this caused his face to actually shine (Exod. 34:28–30). Of course, there has never been such mighty works done by God through a man as the ten plagues of Egypt (Exod. 6:6; 7–12). God also gave him the Ten Commandments (Exod. 20). God said this about Moses: "For thou hast found grace in my sight, and I know thee by name" (Exod. 33:17).

» Joshua was a military general and the great leader of millions of people (Exod. 17:10; Deut. 31:7; 34:9; Josh. 2:24; 8:3–4; 11:12). He had to fill some big shoes, as he took over for Moses. He obeyed the strategy of God to march around Jericho, and not fight, and the walls fell down. At another time he wanted more light in order to win the battle. He was fighting against five kings and their armies, so he "spake...to the LORD...and he said in the sight of Israel, Sun, stand thou still." He commanded the sun to not go down—right in front of all of them. And God did it for him (Josh. 10:12–14). That was bold, as he was confident in the Lord. He was also said of the Lord to be full of the spirit of wisdom, and the Lord magnified him (Num. 27:18; Josh. 4:14; 34:9).

» David was a brilliant military strategist (he killed his ten thousands [1 Sam. 18:7–8]). He was bold and brave, as he fought off a lion and a bear (1 Sam. 17:34–37). He also boldly declared that he would slay Goliath, and told him he would take his head. And he did (vv. 45–46). He is considered the greatest king to ever rule Israel. First Samuel 18:14 states, "And David behaved himself wisely in all his ways;

and the LORD was with him." The Bible states that the throne of David is established forever, and Jesus is the offspring of David (1 Kings 2:45; Rev. 22:16). David was said by God to be a "man after mine own heart" (Acts 13:22).

» King Solomon was the wisest and wealthiest man to ever live, or will ever live (2 Chron. 1:12; 1 Kings 3:12–13; 4:29–30). Second Chronicles 9:1–6 states, "And when the queen of Sheba heard of the fame of Solomon, she came to prove Solomon with hard questions at Jerusalem, with a very great company.... And Solomon told her all her questions: and there was nothing hid from Solomon which he told her not. And when the queen of Sheba had seen the wisdom of Solomon, and the house that he had built... [and all the rest of what he had]... she said to the king, It was a true report... and, behold, the one half of the greatness of thy wisdom was not told me: for thou exceedest the fame that I heard."

» Daniel was a prime minister and of royal descent. He had great wisdom and skill in all learning given by God, more than ten times the wisest in all the land (Dan. 1:3–6, 17, 20; 2:48). He had an excellent spirit and was preferred above all the presidents and princes, and also by King Darius (Dan. 6:2–3). Daniel believed and trusted in God, and God delivered him from the den of lions (Dan. 6:16–26).

» The prophets spent much of their time in prayer to God, who alone is the giver of true wisdom (James 1:5). The prophets also spent time with the king and other rulers, who were, for the most part, not ignorant people. Many did great exploits for God, and they counseled the kings with wisdom from above.

» Matthew was a tax collector (Matt. 9:9) and, of course, he wrote the Book of Matthew. Jesus had dinner at his house one night (Matt. 9:10).

» Luke was "the beloved physician" (Col. 4:14), and he wrote the Gospel of Luke and the Book of Acts.

» Paul was a rabbi and trained by the most educated teacher of his day, Gamaliel (Acts 5:34; 22:3). He wrote two-thirds of the New Testament. Most scholars state that his writings are so intelligently written, so as to not compare to any of the greatest writers of all time. Of course, all the words of the Bible are inspired by God (2 Tim. 3:16).

The Bible states that "the fear of the LORD is the beginning of wisdom" (Prov. 9:10). Someone might be educated—or even brilliant. But if they do not believe in God, they do not have even the beginning of wisdom (James 3:13–17).

Why are we, as educated people, willing to talk about almost any subject, except for the Bible? If we don't talk about a subject and do not investigate it, we will remain ignorant and uninformed. Why would we be resistant in regard to gaining knowledge on something that involves our eternal destiny? Also, why does the mention of the Bible cause many people to even get angry? If it is all just a fairy tale written by uneducated people, then why do so many strive to eliminate it from society? I can tell you why. It is because the Bible convicts people of their sin. Many do not want to be told that what they are doing is a sin. They state that it puts them on a guilt trip. Well, that's just the point! We are all guilty. We all need a Savior, as we all sin (Ps. 51:1–5; 143:2; Rom. 3:10, 12, 23; 5:12; Gal. 3:22).

Many will admit they are dealing with "issues," but please don't call it a "sin," they say. Well, Jesus called it sin (John 5:14; 8:11; 16:8). Calling it a sin makes us all accountable and guilty before the supreme authority, God Almighty. Charles Finney wrote, "All men know that they have sinned, but all are not convicted of the guilt and ill dessert of it."[20]

If people could only understand that what God is instructing us to do is for our own good! The commandments of God are not to restrict us, but rather to protect us and liberate us.

Billy Graham said, "The Ten Commandments tell us not to covet or lust. However, all moral law is more than a test; it is for our own good. Every law which God has given is for our benefit. If a person breaks it, he is not only rebelling against God, he is hurting himself. God gave 'the law' because he loves man. It is for man's benefit. God's commandments were given to protect and promote man's happiness, not to restrict it."[21]

A. W. Tozer said, "Men and women reject this message for the same reason they have rejected all of the Bible. They do not wish to be under the authority of the moral Word of God."[22]

Charles Colson states, "Christianity gives an absolute moral law that allows us to judge between right and wrong.... Without moral absolutes, there is no real basis for ethics. An absolute moral law doesn't confine people in a straitjacket of Victorian prudery. People will always debate the boundaries of moral law and its varied applications. But the very idea of right and wrong makes sense only if there is a final standard, a measuring rod, by which we can make moral judgments."[23]

The wisest man who ever lived was King Solomon (2 Chron. 1:12), except for Jesus, and Solomon was also the wealthiest man to ever live. He recognized the priceless and incomparable value of God's Word above anything else. He had accomplished more than any other human being in history, and he had experienced all of what life had to offer. Finally, toward the end of his life, he made a very wise statement. He said in Ecclesiastes 12:13: "Let us hear the conclusion of the whole matter: Fear God, and keep his commandments: for this is the whole duty of man." A truly profound statement! Yet, most do not adhere to his insightful advice. He wrote much in the Book of Proverbs about the importance of following God's Word—both personally and as a society. David also wrote many verses in regard to the same. Here are some of those verses:

Psalm 33:12: "Blessed is the nation whose God is the LORD."

Psalm 122:6: "Pray for the peace of Jerusalem: they shall prosper that love thee." As a nation, we will prosper if we continue to support Israel (Gen. 12:3).

Proverbs 11:11: "The good influence of godly citizens causes a city to prosper, but the moral decay of the wicked drives it downhill" (TLB).

See also Proverbs 11:14; 14:34; 16:7; 18:15; 20:26, 28; 28:4; 29:2; and Isaiah 66:10–14.

Now, what exactly are the commandments of God that Solomon referred to? God's commandments are summed up in these few verses that Jesus spoke. He said in Matthew 22:37–40: "Thou shalt love the Lord thy God with all thy heart, and with all thy soul, and with all thy mind. This is the first and great commandment. And the second is like unto it, Thou shalt love thy neighbor as thyself. On these two commandments hang all the law and the prophets." If we truly love our neighbor, then we would treat them as we would want to be treated. The Golden Rule, as it is!

The fear of the Lord that King Solomon mentioned is to seek after godly wisdom, knowledge, and understanding, to read His Word daily, and to obey His commandments (Deut. 6:1–9; 17:3; Josh. 1:8; Ps. 119:63; Prov. 2:2; 4:4–8). Many people simply refuse to submit to God. William Penn wrote, "Those who will not be governed by God will be ruled by tyrants."[24]

If we would be humble enough to admit we sin, ask for forgiveness, and acknowledge Jesus as our Lord and Savior, then we are assured of our future entrance into heaven. Jesus Himself said in John 14:6, "I am the way, the truth and the life: no man cometh unto the Father, but by me." He said He was the only way. If we want to live at His house, we must do it His way. Because He loves us, He gives us a free will to choose (Deut. 30:19). You know, all of us are only a heartbeat away from eternity. I urge you to think about this, as there are no second chances once you're in the graveyard. The question I have for you is this: Will you gamble your eternal soul on your opinion, or will you trust in God's Word? What will you decide?

# 5

# Near-Death Experiences

M ANY PEOPLE DO not want to discuss the afterlife. They will carefully plan their few short retirement years, yet they put no effort into researching where they might spend eternity.

Maurice Rawlings, MD, said, "Most people are deathly afraid of dying. They say, 'Doctor, I'm afraid of dying.' But I have never heard one of them say, 'Doctor, I'm afraid of judgment.' And judgment is the main concern of patients who have been there and returned to tell about it."[1]

There are literally thousands of these people, from all different walks of life, who have experienced heaven or hell through near-death experiences. They are too numerous to simply discount as a figment of the imagination or a hallucination.

## A Doctor on His Deathbed

There was a medical doctor, Donald Whitaker, PhD, who was a specialist in research science. He was dying in the hospital. He had only one Christian friend who would tell him about Jesus, but he wasn't interested. The doctor said: "I had a condition that was called acute hemorrhagic necrotic pancreatitis. You don't live with this disease....I was an atheist. You see, it's very easy to be an atheist when you're successful. You have worked your way from Oklahoma welfare to being one of the most powerful men in your part of the country, one of the most powerful men in the state of Oklahoma in relationship to political. It's very easy to be an atheist when you have done all that. Man can sit back and say, 'I don't need God, what is God?' But it's very difficult to be an atheist when you're laying on your deathbed. Because you begin to think, 'What if these people (Christians) are right?'…When I'm laying on my deathbed and knowing that I'm going to die, guess who I thought about. I thought about, 'What if Ron is right? What if there is a heaven and a hell?'…Immediately, *immediately*, the most pressing thought in my mind is, 'How do I get saved? What is saved? What *is* saved? How do I get saved?' And so I sent them for Ron.…I knew that he had something that I had to have.…Ron wasn't home. So I had them send for Ron. That night as I was laying there in bed, I would begin to fade away, and as I would fade away, it was like darkness.…It was so, so dark.…The darkness penetrated into your very being. I can tell you I left my body, because I remember when I came back into my body. I don't know where I was out of my body. There are people that talk about a light…or…floating above…a feeling of warmth and love. I didn't feel any of that. I felt none of that. I felt untold terror, untold terror, because I knew that if I ever went all the way, if I slipped all the way, I would never get back. Now, in my beings of beings, I knew that."

He fought all night long because he knew he had to wait until Ron got there. And the next morning Ron came and led him in the sinner's prayer. This was a very staunch atheist who was wealthy and successful, a very difficult man to convince. But his experience of heading toward hell changed his mind in a hurry.[2]

## A Pilot's Destiny

Another amazing near-death experience is told by a pilot by the name of Captain Dale Black. He was a pilot for TWA, and he flew for over forty years. He has a family, and he has accomplished much in his life. His doctor also verifies the medical claims he makes in his book. His near-death experience happened forty years before he finally shared his story in his book. It is a miracle that he survived the plane crash—and he was the only one who did. His injuries were so massive and extensive, it is a continued miracle that he ever recovered. Here is some of what he saw in heaven:

> I was fast approaching a magnificent city, golden and gleaming, among a myriad of resplendent colors…I was overwhelmed by its beauty.…There was a huge gathering of angels and people, millions, countless millions.…Below me lay the purest, most perfect grass…colorful wild flowers.…The fragrance that permeated heaven was so gentle and sweet.…In the distance stood a range of mountains, majestic in appearance.…It was something like being in a 3-D movie…multiply that by ten thousand.…Utterly breathtaking. My body was elevated above the ground and moved effortlessly.…My energy seemed boundless…even though I had always worked hard to be in excellent condition, I had never come close to feeling as strong and healthy as I felt now. It was as though I could accomplish anything.…Music was everywhere. The worship of God was the heart and focus of the music, and everywhere the joy of the music could be felt…a seamless blend of vocals and instrumentals.…I had never felt such overwhelming peace.…When I had questions or needed understanding, it seemed to be imparted automatically and directly into my heart.…I understood in my heart that God's will was perfection and His Word was the source of all creation.…The Word of God was and is the foundation for everything.

God was the heart of heaven, His love, His will, His order.[3]

There was much more he saw and describes in his book. He states that he has served God fully since the accident, and after his career at TWA he went on to fly thousands of missionaries on their trips and help many other people. He has a PhD in business. "He is a former aircraft systems instructor for the Boeing 747....He founded and operated a jet pilot training and jet aircraft sales company." His list of accomplishments goes on and on.[4]

## A Thrill Seeker

Another former atheist whom my wife, Annette, and I have had the pleasure to meet is Mickey Robinson. He has written a book about his near-death experience. He was an expert parachutist, and he spent his life jumping out of planes and doing other daring adventures. One day, however, the plane crashed. He barely survived, and he had third-degree burns over three-quarters of his body. The doctors were certain he wouldn't make it. During the time he was fading in and out of consciousness and near death, he stepped out of his broken body. He said this:

> I began traveling toward a pure white light, brighter than a thousand suns....But then, as my whole being yearned for this brilliance, I became aware of something moving in behind me....I felt an eerie blackness hovering....The darkness that encompassed me was something more terrifying than evil. This was total emptiness, waiting to penetrate and swallow all that made me alive. And I was helpless, totally incapable of saving myself....I experienced an agony more terrible than being burned

alive. I knew if the darkness swallowed me, I would be imprisoned in an empty world with no windows and no door. I would cry for help, yet never be heard.... And this aloneness would be final, nonnegotiable, never-ending, forever. Shivering in terror, I watched the last eclipse of light disappearing. Then, like a drowning man gasping for air, my spirit screamed out the same words I'd prayed that night in intensive care: 'God, I'm sorry! I want to live! Please give me another chance!'... And just as they escaped my lips, I found myself standing in heaven...a living, breathing glory enfolded me.... And although I could not see any form or shape, I knew it was a Person. The magnificence of this Person pierced me like a laser...all Power, all Wisdom, all Splendor, all Love.... Nothing mattered except to remain in this presence.... Love drenched me like a flood...this pure being clothed in perfect light.[5]

He was shown some of heaven and more, but he didn't want to come back. God sent him back. He recovered, but he had to have many operations. The doctors didn't expect him to make it. He became a Christian and has served God ever since. He now has an international speaking ministry.

## One Wrong Drink!

There was another man my wife and I met who had a near-death experience. Prior to this experience, he was an atheist. His name is B. W. Melvin, and now he is a Christian. His story, told in detail in his book, goes like this:

It was hot working on the outskirts of Tucson during that summer of 1980. One day the temperature...read 124 degrees.... I decided to get a drink of water…a cooler in the back of his truck…I took the first drink: a long, long guzzle. It seemed a bit warm and slimy.…We opened the top of the cooler and looked inside. Green fungus and fuzzy worm-like creatures were swimming around in a putrid clear green-brown muck.[6]

He became horrified. He later became deathly sick, said he was in agony, with vomiting and a high fever, that caused him to feel so very cold. Some hours later he suddenly left his body and floated through the ceiling. He began going down a tunnel in extreme darkness, but there was an astounding light in the distance. As he approached this light, he saw it was emitted from a man in a white robe.

The beauty of the light awed me.…When He revealed a hand, rays of brightness came forth in blinding fashion.…My fate appeared sealed before arriving here. *I was without excuse.*[7]

He said he was told by the Lord Jesus that he would see "and walk amidst an unknown land best forgotten but not left unseen."[8]

He saw unspeakable horror, smelled a stench that was extremely putrid, heard intense screams, saw flames, and felt intense heat. He saw demons tormenting people in cages, and he was terrified and felt hopelessly lost forever. Then the Lord came and took him out of that horrid place. A friend found him later, and suddenly he came back to life. He was taken to the hospital, was treated, and eventually recovered. He had contracted a deadly waterborne illness.

The doctor…turning to me he said, "Mr. Melvin, you have contracted Vibrio Cholerae and have passed the critical stage. You are lucky."[9]

His book gives a great description of all he saw in hell, and it will terrify anyone. It caused him to become a believer in Jesus Christ as his Lord and Savior.

## A Spiral Downward

Perry Stone shares in his book the story of someone he had met who, in 1974, was dying at the hospital. He had a near-death experience, in which he was headed toward hell. His name was Bill Fishel. Perry states that…

…he was aware of moving rapidly into a dark tunnel…going downward into the floor and under the crust of the earth. He described this tunnel as very "dreary and dark." His first question to himself was, "If I died, then why am I not going up toward heaven?"…As he continued his descent, spiraling downward, he observed a faint light at the end of the long tunnel….The light, he would later learn, was coming from a large cavern somewhere in the earth….He described an intense heat….The ground was desolate and hard….He noticed that people of various ages began to appear….Bill would later realize these were the souls and spirits of men and women from around the world who had just passed away on Earth and were all drawn to this area before their final confinement….

The entire mass of people began moving slowly toward this supernatural being. Suddenly it was as if a veil was lifted, and Bill began seeing these people falling headlong into a very large opening that he described as a "massive pit."…He observed a second angelic-looking creature casting people into this immeasurable opening….The huge canyon contained thousands of smaller pits, all burning with fire….He suddenly heard a mighty chorus of moans and cries arising from below.... Bill said, "There was a very depressing darkness far above the hole, and a strong odor in the air of burning sulfur"...and the sickening smell of burnt flesh...he began crying out to God for mercy and help.

Meanwhile, in the hospital the doctor and nurses were working on reviving Bill and were successful. In the place he acknowledges as hell, he was suddenly being drawn back upward toward the earth's surface....I asked Bill, "Were you attending church when this happened?" He replied, "I would go to church, but I was not living the life I should. But after this incident, I was so shaken that I said I would serve the Lord and follow Him all of my life." Bill certainly was faithful and did follow the Lord until his death.[10]

## A View of Hell and a Warning From a Lost Soul!

Another man was interviewed on Christian television. His name is Ron Reagan. His story is powerful. He was once an atheist. He had done some terrible things in his younger years, and he had kept some very bad company. He had been down a very tough road. One day he walked into a store and got into a fight. The other man cut his arm open with a broken bottle, and he began to bleed to death. He was on his way to the hospital in an ambulance, when suddenly he began to leave his body. He said:

> The ambulance looked like it had exploded, like it had blown up. Suddenly I was going through a tunnel. And after some period of time, coming out of the smoke, out of darkness, I began to hear the voices of a multitude of people. They were screaming,

groaning, and crying. As I looked down, the sensation was [like] looking down upon a volcanic opening, seeing fire, smoke, and people screaming, crying. They were burning, but not being consumed.... The most terrible part of it, I began to recognize many of the people I was seeing in these flames. I could see their features; I could see the frustration and the pain. And a number of them began to call my name, saying, "Ronnie, don't come to this place. If you come here, there's no escape. There's no way out." I looked into the face of one who had been shot in a robbery attempt and bled to death. I saw others I knew who had died of overdose. [I saw] the agony and the pain they were experiencing. The most powerful part of it was the loneliness, that there was no hope, there was no escape. The smell was so foul, like sulfur, like an electric welder, and the stench was terrible.[11]

He said he had experienced about everything terrible that life had to offer in his lifetime, and he had seen many horrible things. But this "literally scared me to death as I'm looking into this pit, this place of torment."[12]

His story is very convincing when you hear him describe his circumstances. We have met him and his wife, and I believe him. They were both very kind and compassionate, and he was a gentle, loving, and sincere man. He accepted the Lord as his Savior shortly after this experience and has been a pastor of a church for many years.[13]

## Stories From Dr. Maurice Rawlings

Maurice Rawlings, MD, has written many books on his studies of near-death experiences. Those who have had visions of the afterlife, and clinically dead individuals who saw heaven, hell, and sometimes simply a bright light, share many of their experiences. Dr. Rawlings has done much research, and his books are fascinating. Here is a brief overview of some of those stories.

> Memorial Hospital in Chattanooga—collected by Mary Ann Hickman and assistant head nurse Dotty Gilbert. They report that Ira Anderson (not his real name), a sixty-two-year-old male suffering an acute heart attack, had to be restrained because, using his words, there were "demons coming after me." Fighting the staff, writhing and kicking off the creatures....After the cardiac arrest rhythm had been corrected by electric shock, the demons seemed to follow him as he went to the intensive care area, where, regaining his consciousness, they pounced on him once again. Review of the records showed no medications to account for the demonization. In the same week and in the same emergency room, Ruby Tinney and charge nurse Nancy Humphries reported a thirty-eight-year-old heart attack victim, who, with bloodcurdling screams, kept yelling he was in hell and demanding that a pastor be called.[14]

Dr. Rawlings continues with another story about Sir Francis Newport, who was on his deathbed and said this: "'Why have I become a skeleton in three or four days? See now, then. I have despised my Maker, and denied my Redeemer. I have joined myself to the atheist and profane, and continued this course under many convictions…when my security was the greatest, and the checks of my conscience were the least.'…In inexpressible horror, he cried out, 'Oh, the insufferable pangs of Hell!' and died at once."[15]

Another of several negative experiences recorded by Shaw included that of Mrs. J. B. in 1886: I called to see her during her last sickness and found her in a most distressing state of mind. She...saying, "Devils are in my room, ready to drag my soul down to hell."...She would say, "See them laugh!" This would throw her into a paroxysm of fear and dread...but when I tried to get her to look to Jesus for help she said, "It is no use; it is too late!"[16]

Dr. Rawlings continues with this: "Napoleon Bonaparte in 1821 confessed to the Count de Montholon:...'Such is the fate of him who has been called the great Napoleon! What an abyss between my deep misery and the eternal kingdom of Christ.'"[17]

Another story from Dr. Rawlings:

And then the self-reliant Voltaire, whose "pen was mightier than the sword," whose intellect and honors could never be excelled, was now excelled by a stroke that was slowly causing his death....For two months he was tortured with such an agony as led him at times to gnash his teeth in impotent rage against God and man....Then, turning his face, he would cry out, "I must die—abandoned of God and of men!"...Even his nurse repeatedly said, "For all the wealth of Europe I would never see another infidel die."[18]

Yet another story by Dr. Rawlings:

Mr. Bartholomy in the nursing home: "What is it you see?" I said. Mr. Bartholomy was trembling and grimacing at something behind me. When I turned, I could see nothing there. "They're coming again!" he repeated. "Who's coming?" I insisted. Mr. Bartholomy was then sitting bolt upright for the first time in a week, but kept looking toward the window. "They're prowling around over there just waiting for me to die. Make them go away!"…I could see that no drugs had been administered, there was no fever, and no lab problem except anemia.…The chart indicated he was well educated, a Protestant, several grandchildren…a little later that night he died.[19]

It doesn't matter what someone's religion is. Many are atheists, and they saw hell. It isn't Christianity that would influence a person's mind to see the biblical hell. Hell is a real place, and it does, in fact, exist. Jesus told us He was the only way to heaven (John 6:40; 8:24; 14:6). Hell has many guests who were lured in by deception, and those guests are permanent. Satan is the great deceiver (Ps. 9:17; 55:15; 63:9; Prov. 7:27; 9:18; 15:24; Isa. 14:12–19; Ezek. 28:12–19; Luke 10:18).

Another experience is written in a book called *To Heaven and Back* by Rita Bennett. She documents many stories of those who have seen heaven or hell. Here is one of those stories of a near-death experience:

Doctors discovered that I had double pneumonia, a blood clot, internal bleeding, and kidney failure.…I heard the doctor in a loud voice asking the nurse to check my blood pressure. I heard the nurse answer, "Zero. Zilch." I realized they were fighting for my life.…I was talking to God and saying, "Why me? Why now?" I didn't want to die.…I started moving upward. I realized my body was below me.…At the first heaven I met a Being.…I recognized him as Jesus Christ, and he led me through the three heavens.…I looked into his eyes. They were piercing but loving and as clear as blue water.…When he looked at you, he looked straight through you and into you. You realized immediately that he knew all there was to know about you.... In a matter of seconds I found myself before the Most High.... Then I heard the Father and Son communing about my case. Jesus said, "My blood is sufficient. She's mine." When he said that, all the doubts about my unworthiness disappeared. I jumped up and down, shouting and rejoicing. I have never been so happy in all my life! The kind of love I felt is beyond explanation. I kept saying, "Oh, my God. Oh, my God. This is my Advocate." Just as I read in the Bible. Jesus came back to where I was and looked at me again with comforting love.... I never wanted to leave his side. I told him so, but a look in his eyes said I had to return.... Coming back into my body in intensive care was as quick as my journey out had been.[20]

She recovered and began a work for the Lord. She said, "When I came back, I had a different appreciation for human relationships. They are so important. Much of what we think of as important isn't important at all.... My strongest sense is that my purpose is to love."[21]

## The Stench of Sulfur

Jerry R. Newberry shares his experience. I also talked with him personally. He called me on the phone after he watched me on a Christian television program. When he was fifteen years of age, he nearly died of appendicitis. He said that after the surgery:

The lights above my bed just slowly went out.... Suddenly, a dim haze appeared and I could see a tunnel!... I could hear, in the distance, people moaning and groaning and wailing. I was very frightened. At that time two hooded beings appeared, one on either side....I had never heard wailing of that magnitude. It was a horrible sound. The other thing that was so bad was the smell. It was like many things burning together. My eyes burned, my nostrils burned, and my lungs burned. We walked into the corridors and there were countless people behind huge metal bars...imagine a place so hot it is unbearable with total hopelessness and despair....I saw thousands and countless thousands of people behind those massive metal bars....I thought I could not stand the odor...(at this time I was not a Christian). I heard a voice with a sound of a total command and authority say, "He has to go back." We made an about-face....I opened my eyes and the light seemed so bright. I slowly looked around. My mother and siblings were all standing at my bedside....I knew I would never be the same again. The very first Sunday I was able, I went to church....At the beginning of the altar call, I went to the altar and gave my heart to Jesus Christ, my King of kings and Lord of lords.[22]

This experience happened to him in 1946, and he didn't write about it until 2006. But he never forgot his horrid experience, and then in 1989 he had a bit of proof for himself as he visited Hawaii. He and his wife visited the volcano crater, and he said, "It hit me like a ton of bricks: This causes the same odor and the burning of the eyes." He remembered all those years ago in 1946, when he had smelled that same foul odor of burning sulfur in hell. God gives us a glimpse of hell with the molten lava and the stench of sulfur of the volcano so that we will avoid this horrible place (Prov. 27:12).

# 6

# Clinical Death Experiences

THIS NEXT STORY is about a man who worked at a sawmill in Oregon back in 1924, fell, and was dead for forty-five minutes. This is actually beyond clinical death.

I landed on my head on the first beam thirty feet down...until I fell into the water and disappeared from view.... The search went on for forty-five minutes to one hour before I was found by Mr. J. H. Gunderson.... I was dead as far as this world is concerned. But I was alive in another world.... The next thing I knew, I was standing near a shoreline of a great ocean of fire. It appeared to be what the Bible says it is in Revelation 21:8, "The lake which burns with fire and brimstone." This is the most awesome sight one could ever see this side of the final judgment. I remember more clearly than any other thing...every detail of every moment.... I was standing some distance from the burning, turbulent, rolling mass of blue fire. As far as my eyes could see it was just the same.... There was nobody in it. I saw other people whom I had known that had died.... We recognized each other.... Their expressions were those of bewilderment and confusion. The scene was so awesome that words simply fail.... There is no way of escape except by Divine intervention. I said to myself in an audible voice, "If

57

I had known about this I would have done anything that was required of me to escape coming to a place like this."…I saw another man coming by in front of us. I knew immediately who it was. He had a strong, kind, compassionate face, composed and unafraid. Master of all He saw. It was Jesus Himself.…I said again to myself, "If He would only look my way and see me, He could rescue me from this place."…He turned His head and looked directly at me. That is all it took. His look was enough. In seconds I was back and entering into my body again.…I thank God for people who can pray. It was Mrs. Brocke I heard praying for me. She said, "O God, don't take Tom. He is not saved."[1]

In Mrs. Brocke's own words recorded in his book, she prayed this prayer:

> We just asked God to be merciful and raise him up. First we saw his eyelids move just a little, then the tears began to come and he tried to talk.…More life came into him and the men standing around were all amazed and happy. They had seen a miracle.…When they got him to the hospital, he was taken into surgery and they cleaned the wounds in his head and put a lot of stitches in his scalp. Seven ribs on his left side were broken; they bandaged him up for that.[2]

This is a well-documented story of Thomas Welch, who had fallen off a timber at a sawmill in Bridal Veil in Oregon in 1924. He was underwater for at least forty-five minutes and found dead. Seeing hell caused him to become a Christian, to study for the ministry, and to serve God for the remainder of his years. He served with people such as Gordon Lindsay.[3]

Dr. Gary L. Wood had an experience that is also quite interesting. He had a car accident and was instantly killed. He states:

> I turned to see what the matter was. There was an explosion, then a sharp, instant pain seared across my face. There was a brilliant light that engulfed me, and I remember being free from all pain. I slipped out of my body.... I was above the car now.... I could see my body.... As I began to ascend up through this tunnel of light, I felt such a tranquil feeling of peace wash over me.... All around me I could hear angels singing.... I then began walking on a green, lush carpet of grass that covered the hillside.... From the hill, I viewed the outer portion of a magnificent city. There was a wonderful wall made of jasper that surrounded the city.... In front of me was a very beautiful gate made of solid pearl that was studded with sapphires, rubies, diamonds, and many other precious gems.... Suddenly, there in front of me stood my best friend, John.... John took me into a very large building that looked like a library. The walls were solid gold.... I saw hundreds and hundreds of volumes of books.... John explained to me that these books contain a record of every person's life that has ever been born, throughout all history. Everything we do here on the earth is recorded in these books—good or bad.... I could see the prayers of the saints below shooting up like arrows towards heaven. Angels would receive the prayers and bring them into the throne room of God. God would grant the prayer request and the angel would be dispatched from the room to deliver the miracle.... I have never seen anyone or anything that could

possibly compare to the beauty of our Lord Jesus, who I now stood before.[4]

Dr. Wood had "broken vertebrae…one of which causes certain death.…He had a mid-face injury with lorinzal injuries, which means his vocal cords and voice box were completely shattered. He was given no hope to ever talk again."[5]
He says:

> I have an X-ray that shows that I have no vocal cords, yet I talk and sing.…I prayed, "God…you can touch me, you can heal me.…I dedicate the rest of my life to tell the world about you." Suddenly, Jesus appeared in my room.…He put his gentle hand on my throat, and I felt warmth flowing through my body.…The nurse walked in and said, "Good morning…" I said, "Good morning." With a startled look on her face, she said, "You can't talk!"…Within moments, I was surrounded by doctors saying…"You can't do it. You should not be able to speak. You have no vocal cords."[6]

Dr. Wood is a living miracle, and he preaches and sings to this day.

Another remarkable experience was that of a fairly well-known preacher, the late Richard Sigmund. His experience was also beyond clinical death.

> He was known as "Little Richard" as a boy preacher and preached in some of the largest meetings in the world at that time: Oral Roberts, A. A. Allen, William Branham, Jack Coe, Kathryn Kuhlman and many more.…On October 17, 1974, Richard had a devastating car accident and was pronounced dead.

Eight hours later, God brought him back to life, but not before he had seen *A Place Called Heaven*....

There were sirens. Lots of noise. And I heard the words, "He's dead." A force was drawing me up through a glory cloud and on the other side of the cloud I could hear people singing.... I could see two women standing. They were beautiful and of great age, but their countenance was as though they were in their mid-twenties.[7]

He saw people waiting for their loved ones to arrive in heaven, and as they did, they would pass through a veil. After passing through the veil, they immediately became young and beautiful. He saw beautiful flowers, grass, and trees of enormous size. He said:

There is no death, not even one blade of grass would die in heaven....As I walked along the golden pathway, I saw the sky. It was rosette pinkish in color but still it was a crystal-clear blue....the clouds were thousands of angels....All the people were in preparation of loved ones coming into heaven....On the right was another book. It was the Lamb's Book of Life....I went up to the wall. The wall was filled with all types of precious jewels....The gates were huge. Twenty-five miles high...through the gate along the pathway were many beautiful houses—mansions....People would casually stroll off the edge of their verandas and very easily float to the ground....I would get a glimpse of Jesus just a bit further ahead. He was talking with people, loving them, hugging them....I wanted to be there just to fall at His feet....I just wanted to be with Jesus....In heaven everybody has his turn and nobody is anxious....A little girl came up to me...and had beautiful blond hair. I knew she had died of cancer....she promptly proceeded to mess up her beautiful hair, hair that she had lost when she suffered from cancer. There were many other children and each had abilities far greater than any adult on earth.[8]

He saw angels being sent to respond to our prayers; he saw mountains, great bodies of water, people, animals, and families; he heard beautiful singing, and many other things in heaven. But the most wonderful experience he had was that of meeting Jesus and seeing the throne of God.

He goes on to say:

Apparently, I had been dead for over eight hours and they were wheeling me down to the morgue....I could feel my bones knitting together. I could feel the scars healing while I sat up....I remember a doctor coming in saying, "I pronounced him dead. And he is dead." But I was sitting up. Other doctors and nurses came in and I began to tell the story of where I had been and what had happened.[9]

God had also shown him hell, and he describes the most horrid sights you can even imagine.

Another testimony comes from the well-known book *90 Minutes in Heaven* by Don Piper. He was a pastor who had just left a church where he was preaching. He was crossing a bridge, when suddenly an out-of-control semitrailer hit him head-on and ran right over the top of his car. He was instantly killed. He was pronounced dead by four paramedics on the scene and continued to remain dead for ninety minutes. His experience also went beyond clinical death. His arm was severed, along with his part of his leg, and he had many other serious problems. He eventually needed thirty-four operations to repair his severe injuries after he came back to life. God brought him back to life, but not until he saw heaven.

His book documents the medical reports and pictures of the accident, hospital records, and such. He is a very credible, sound, and successful person whom my wife and I have had the opportunity to spend time with. We have spoken together, and I believe his story. This is what he said:

> In one powerful, overwhelming second, I died.... Simultaneous with my last recollection of seeing the bridge and the rain, a light enveloped me, with brilliance beyond earthly comprehension or description.... In my next moments of awareness, I was standing in heaven. Joy pulsated through me as I looked around, and at that moment I became aware of a large crowd of people.... They rushed toward me, and every person was smiling, shouting, and praising God.... I felt overwhelmed by the number of people who had come to welcome me to heaven.... As I looked around, I could hardly grasp the vivid, dazzling colors.... I had the sense that I was being ushered into the presence of God.... A holy awe came over me.... My most vivid memory of heaven is what I heard.... It was the most beautiful and pleasant sound I've ever heard.... The melodies of praise filled the atmosphere.... I was home.... I wanted to be there more than I had ever wanted to be anywhere on earth.... I did not see God. Although I knew God was there.... [There was] an awesome gate interrupting a wall that faded out of sight in both directions.... As I gazed upward, I couldn't see the top either.... I could see inside. It was like a city with paved streets. To my amazement, they had been constructed of literal gold.... My

friends and relatives were all in front of me, calling, urging, and inviting me to follow…just outside the gate…I was in heaven and ready to go in through the pearlescent gate.…Then, just as suddenly as I had arrived at the gates of heaven, I left them.…The EMTs pronounced me dead as soon as they arrived at the scene. They stated that I died instantly.[10]

He had been dead for ninety minutes. A couple who were at the same church where Don had just spoken was on the same road going home. They were stopped in the backed-up traffic, so they got out of their car, walked up, and asked the police officer if they could pray for anyone. The officer told them that the man in the red car was deceased. They asked the officer if they could pray for him. He said, "Well, you know, if that's what you want to do, go ahead, but I've got to tell you it's an awful sight. He's dead, and it's really a mess under that tarp. Blood and glass are everywhere, and the body's all mangled." The pastor, Dick, went to pray. He said, "I felt compelled to pray. I didn't know who the man was or whether he was a believer. I knew only that God told me I had to pray for him." He prayed for a while, and then he started singing a song. He was singing, "What a Friend We Have in Jesus." Then suddenly the dead man began to sing with him. He immediately "scrambled out of the smashed car and raced over to the nearest EMT." They wouldn't believe him, that the dead man was now alive. It took Dick a while to persuade them to go and see. Well, long story short, Don miraculously recovered and today speaks all over the world.[11]

Another experience is reported by Dr. Maurice Rawlings:

[There was a man whose] high blood pressure caused repeated heart attacks, which in turn caused repeated episodes of fibrillation and sudden clinical death.... "Everything was turning black. My heart stopped beating! I heard the nurses shouting, 'Code 99, Code 99!' One of them dialed the phone to the hospital loudspeaker.... I could feel myself leaving my body...floating in the air.... Then I was lightly standing on my feet watching the nurses push down on my chest. Two more nurses came in and one was wearing a rose on her uniform. Two more nurses came in and one orderly and then I noticed they had gotten my doctor back.... Then my doctor took off his coat to relieve the nurse pushing on my chest. I noticed he had on a blue-striped tie."[12]

He was brought back to life, and Dr. Rawlings explains:

The specific things the patient saw, including the number of people, what they did, and what they were wearing were subsequently verified. Reconstruction of the time sequence indicated that he was without heartbeat or consciousness during this entire interval of recall.[13]

The doctor went on to tell about another time this man had died. This time he saw what appeared to be heaven:

"The next thing I knew I was floating at the far end of the room.... I was flying through space at a rapid rate. There was a river below me.... I was crossing over a beautiful city below.... The streets seemed to be made of shining gold and were wonderfully beautiful.... I descended onto one of the streets and people were all around me—happy people who were glad to see me.... Some other people were coming toward me. I think they were my parents. But just then I woke up, back in the hospital room. I was back in my body. This time I really wished they hadn't brought me back." This patient…said he was a Christian.[14]

Dr. Richard Eby shares an experience he had when he died. He also was beyond clinical death. He had fallen off a balcony and split his head open. He states:

> The bloody skull was exposed with the scalp torn down over each ear. The body was already grey-white and the blood had quit flowing.[15]

His wife checked his pulse and breath and there was none. Dr. Eby explains what he was experiencing. He states:

> In the twinkling of an eye, Jesus took me out of this world.…All this time I was instinctively aware that the Lord of Lords was everywhere about this place.…My gaze riveted on the exquisite valley.…Forests and symmetrical trees…not a brown spot or dead leaf…stately grasses.…I discovered there was no time lag between thought and act.…I had been aware of the most beautiful, melodious, angelic background music.…I bent again and smelled the flowers.…A perfume so exotic…I decided to find my wife and share this unbelievable peace and joy. It seemed only natural that she must have died also, since marriage had made the twain one. Instantly again I found myself going down the path, effortless, weightless, and confident. As the bend in the valley floor approached, I heard her distant voice calling, "Richard, Richard…" As the voice grew louder, the valley grew dimmer, and the light went out.…Later I would realize that I was back on earth where the prayers of many had been answered for my return.…Somehow my

skull had been split apart enough to shift the eye sockets....Around noon the surgeon appeared: "Don't get false hopes, Doc! There is no way to avoid being a vegetable. Your brain tissue yesterday was jelly where we saw it exposed. You had no blood left, so we couldn't transfuse you....I don't know why you're still here. It beats me." I know, Jesus told me I would live![16]

It was a miracle he recovered. He went on sharing his testimony and serving God until he finally went home to be with the Lord in the nineties. Dr. Eby was a very accomplished doctor.

Dr. Kenneth E. Hagin shares an actual death experience he had when he was seventeen years of age. At the age of fifteen, he became bedfast with two serious organic heart problems. The doctors gave him absolutely no hope. He shares:

Earlier that evening my heart had stopped beating and the spiritual man who lives in my body had departed....I went down, down, down until the lights of the earth faded away....I have proof that I was actually dead....The farther down I went, the blacker it became...the hotter and more stifling it became. Finally, far below me, I could see lights flickering on the walls of the caverns of the damned. The lights were caused by the fires of hell....The heat beat me in the face....I came to the entrance of hell....I sensed that one more foot, one more step, one more yard, and I would be gone forever and could not come out of that horrible place! Upon reaching the bottom of the pit, I became conscious of some kind of spirit being by my side....The creature laid his hand on my arm to escort me in. At that same moment, a voice spoke from far above the blackness, above the earth, above the heavens....When he spoke, his words reverberated throughout the region of the damned, shaking it like a leaf in the wind, and causing the creature to take his hand off my arm....I began to ascend until I came to the top of the pit and saw the lights of earth.[17]

This happened three times, each time with Dr. Hagin returning to his body. The third time he had said:

As I began to descend in the darkness this third time, my spirit cried out, "God, I belong to the church! I've been baptized in water!" I waited for Him to answer, but no answer came....It will take more than church membership—it will take more than being baptized in water—to miss hell and make heaven. Jesus said, "...*Ye must be born again*" (John 3:7).[18]

He reached the bottom of the pit again, and the creature grabbed him again. The voice spoke, and the creature let him go again. This time, as he began rising in the tunnel, he said this:

I began to pray, "O God! I come to You in the Name of the Lord Jesus Christ. I ask You to forgive me of my sins and to cleanse me from all sin." I came up beside the bed....I looked at the clock and saw it was 20 minutes before 8 o'clock. That was the very hour I was born again due to the mercy of God through the prayers of my mother. I felt wonderful— it was just like a two-ton weight had rolled off my chest.[19]

Dr. Hagin began to recover from his heart condition. He became the founder of Rhema Bible Institute, served the Lord his entire life, and preached almost every day until he went home to be with the Lord at a good old age.

In many of the books written about these experiences, the majority mention a good experience, such as seeing a bright light, feelings of love and warmth, and peace. Why are there not more of the bad experiences reported?

Dr. Maurice Rawlings says this:

> Some of the "good" experiences could have been false impressions, perhaps created by Satan appearing as an "angel of light." [See 2 Corinthians 11:14.] Or perhaps the meeting place is a pleasant environment representing "sorting ground" or a pre-judgment area, since most cases report a barrier that prevents progress in the beyond. The patient returns to his body before the barrier can be transversed.…, I have found that most of the bad experiences are soon suppressed deeply into the patient's subliminal or subconscious mind. These bad experiences seem to be so painful and disturbing that they are removed from the conscious recall.[20]

It is interesting that Dr. Rawlings also noted:

> I don't know of any "good" out-of-the-body experiences that have resulted from suicide.… Here is an account described by one of my colleagues: She took a bottle of aspirin…in a coma…she kept saying, "Mama, help me! Make them let go of me! They're trying to hurt me!"…"Them, those demons in hell…" She subsequently became a missionary several years later.[21]

# 7

# Dreams and Visions
# of the Afterlife

THE BIBLE MENTIONS many who had dreams or visions throughout its pages. If someone has an authentic dream or vision from God, then it will line up with Scripture. If the person says anything that is contrary to the Bible, then it is not from God. There have been many I have talked with or have read their book, and there are things said that are unbiblical. Yet many believe them to be from God. We must be careful to weigh every account alongside the Word of God. If someone's experience doesn't line up with the Word of God, then it should be discarded.

In light of that there are also those who have had a legitimate experience from God. The Bible states in Joel 2:28 that in the last days "your old men shall dream dreams, your young men shall see visions." (See also Acts 2:17.) It is a scriptural promise that there will be people having dreams and visions. Paul had the vision of Jesus when he saw only a bright light and heard the voice of Jesus on the road to Damascus. This was prior to him becoming a Christian (Acts 9:3–7). Again, Paul had another vision of heaven (2 Cor. 12:1–4) "and heard unspeakable words, which it is not lawful for a man to utter." He might have actually died in this vision, scholars don't know, but it was a vision as he stated. Paul had another vision in Acts 18:9: "Then spake the Lord to Paul in the night by a vision..." John was taken to heaven in a vision (Rev.

4:1; 9:17) and saw many things. Stephen saw Jesus standing on the throne of God in heaven (Acts 7:55–56) right before they stoned him to death for his belief and stand for Jesus. Cornelius had a vision of an angel telling him to send men to Joppa to see Peter (Acts 10:1–7). Peter had a vision where he "saw heaven opened, and a certain vessel descending unto him…" (Acts 10:10–16). In Jonah 2:2 the prophet saw a glimpse of hell. He used the word, "Sheol," which is the Hebrew word for the place of departed spirits. He said, "Out of the belly of hell (Sheol) cried I." There are several commentaries that state that Jonah actually saw hell (Sheol), and I quoted them in my book *Hell*.[1]

There are many who have seen hell. I was shown hell in a vision for the purpose of informing others of the way to avoid that horrid place. I am only a signpost to point people to the Bible, to check out the scriptures for themselves, so they can avoid that terrible place of torment. There are many verses in the Bible describing hell. I document them in my three books: *23 Minutes in Hell*, *Hell*, and *23 Questions About Hell*. If you think hell is a joke, there will come a time when you will greatly regret your cynicism.

I did not have a near-death experience; I had an out-of-body experience, which is classified as a "vision" in the Bible. In 2 Corinthians 12:1–2 Paul, when he was caught up to heaven in a vision, said, "Whether in the body, I cannot tell; or whether out of the body, I cannot tell…" He didn't know, so it would be wrong to say it is not possible. I viewed my body lying on the floor, so I knew I had left my body, and upon returning, I reentered my body. In a vision it is possible to travel, as Paul and John did, to heaven in their spirit body (1 Cor. 15:44). Ezekiel was picked up by his hair and carried to Jerusalem in a vision (Ezek. 8:3). In Genesis 15:1–5 the Lord took Abraham in a vision and "brought him forth abroad."

In Acts 12:9 Peter, when he was released from prison, thought he was in a vision. He actually was released, but he couldn't distinguish a vision from reality. This is because a vision is just as real as physical life itself. God can take someone in a vision to wherever He pleases. There are many who have seen heaven or hell, and hundreds have been documented in books and even more have not been. There are also many more dreams and visions recorded in the Bible.

Dr. Erwin Lutzer said, "If Stephen saw our Lord before he died, and if Paul died and was caught up into paradise, it is just possible that other believers might also have such a vision."[2]

Dr. Norvel Hayes states regarding visions: "But there is a great deal of emphasis on this subject in the Bible, and great respect should be shown for any ministry of the Holy Spirit, including visions."[3]

In all of these stories the people had experienced very similar things.

## More Experiences

John Bunyan, born in 1628, wrote a book called *Visions of Heaven and Hell*. He is well-known for his famous book called *The Pilgrim's Progress*, and he was a respected preacher and pastor of the Baptist church in Bedford, England. He is considered very credible and reputable. He writes about an angel who appeared to him and said, "Fear not, for I am sent to show you things you have not seen." He said:

> I found myself far above the earth.... When I was first brought near this glorious place, I saw innumerable hosts of bright attendants, who welcomed me into that blissful seat of happiness.... All that light, which flows with so much transparent brightness throughout those heavenly mansions, is nothing but

emanations of the divine glory, In comparison, the light of the sun is but darkness.[4]

The angel said to him:

Death does not enter within this blessed place.... Neither sin nor sorrow have anything to do here, for it is the glory of this happy place to be forever freed from all that is evil.[5]

He saw people there, and even a friend who had passed away. He conversed with him, and many things about heaven were explained to him. He was also shown hell.

We were soon surrounded with a darkness much blacker than night. It was attended with a stench more suffocating by far than that of burning brimstone. Likewise, my ears were filled with horrid yellings of the damned spirits.... Now we were within hell's territories, placed in the caverns of the infernal deep. There, where earth's center adjusts all things...we...saw two wretched souls tormented by a fiend, who without ceasing plunged them in liquid fire and burning brimstone.... We saw one who had flaming sulfur forced down her throat by a tormenting spirit.... We saw a wretched soul almost choked with brimstone lying on a bed of burning steel. He cried out as one suffering dreadful anguish.[6]

The man in anguish said:

How often was I pressed to leave those paths of sin that would be sure to bring me to the chambers of eternal death! But I, like the deaf adder, lent no ear.... Salvation was offered to me, but I refused it…but it was offered to me a thousand times; yet, wretch that I was, I still as often refused it. O cursed sin, that with deluding pleasures bewitches mankind to eternal ruin![7]

John continues on to see much more horror and describes it in detail.

## Perry Stone's Vision

In Perry Stone's book, he said:

I am uncertain if it was a dream or a vision.…I looked around and saw in the distance various types of architecture…a massive white stone building that reminded me of the Greco-Roman buildings we see in drawings and paintings…I saw…a massive, very contemporary city with large skyscrapers.…The entire city was an emerald green.…I was told that this area was for those who had passed away and had lived in major cities during their lives.…I looked to my left and recognized a young man who had been converted to Christ in my ministry. During his lifetime this young man wore a back brace; he had been deformed from birth. He shouted out at me and said, "Perry! Perry! Look at me…I no longer wear that brace! I can bend and move without pain! Look at me!" I hugged him, and we rejoiced together.[8]

The experience continues with some astonishing remarks and things seen, but you will have to get his book to read about them.

Erwin W. Lutzer shares a story in his book:

Judson B. Palmer relates the story of the Reverend A. D. Sandborn, who preceded him as pastor in a church in Iowa. Reverend Sandborn called on a young Christian woman who was seriously ill…looking off in the distance, "Now just as soon as they open the gate I will go in," she whispered. Then she sank upon her pillow in disappointment. "They have let Mamie go in ahead of me, but soon I will go in." Moments later she again spoke, "They let Grampa in ahead of me, but next time I will go in for sure." No one spoke to her and she said nothing more to anyone, and seemed to see nothing except the sights of the beautiful city. Reverend Sandborn then left the house because of the press of other duties. Later in the day the pastor learned that the young woman had died that morning. He was so impressed with what she had said that he asked the family about the identity of Mamie and Grampa. Mamie was a little girl who had lived near them at one time but later moved to New York State. As for Grampa, he was a friend of the family and had moved somewhere in the southwest. Reverend Sandborn then wrote to the addresses given him to inquire about these two individuals. Much to his astonishment he discovered that both Mamie and Grampa had died the morning of September 16, the very hour that the young woman herself had passed into glory. Death is not the end of the road; it is only a *bend* in the road.[9]

Another person whom my wife and I have met is Lori Haider, who wrote the book *Saved From Hell*. She had a very promising career after graduating college and was doing quite well. However, she had struggled in her spiritual life since she was a child. At one point she had become a psychic, as she had been attracted to spiritual matters. However, it was the wrong direction to go. She became immersed in the New Age movement and teaching psychic development. Lori said:

> I spent several thousands of dollars buying New Age and world religions books....I was determined to understand Hinduism, Buddhism, Native American spirituality, psychic development, astrology, and the history of all the world religions....The words "Satan" or "demons" were never mentioned. At this time, I didn't understand that Satan, demons, or hell were real....I had studied so many world religions, that Jesus got lumped in with all of the other gods. Eventually, I reached a point where I didn't know what was true and if there really was a God.[10]

She periodically would see demons and be harassed by them. She became confused and depressed to the point of deciding to commit suicide. One day, she said, just before she was going to kill herself:

> Something unexpected happened. A figure that radiated gold light walked up to me and said, "Everything you think that can only heal when you die, I can help you with here."[11]

She said He reached out His hand to her and said:

> You just have to say yes to me.[12]

She went on to say:

> My plans for death were jerked out from under me....I looked at Jesus and said "yes." Here was Jesus who I had rejected so many times in my life coming to me once again.[13]

One day during a church service that she was attending with a friend, she felt strongly that she was to repent of her sins. She had not done so. After the service she was with her friend and fell ill. She said:

> [I] felt as though something had grabbed me on the side of my head. The pain was so intense that I suddenly had to lie down.... Inside my spirit, I heard the words, *brain aneurism*.[14]

Her friend began praying for her. She states that:

> Then, I began seeing into the spirit realm.... [I saw this reptilian creature with] one of its claws on and in my head.[15]

She saw a prison cell in hell that was for her. Fire was closing in on the cell, and soon the cell would be engulfed in the flames.

> I was horrified when I realized that I would repeatedly experience being burned alive, yet never able to die.... About ten sinister-looking demons were standing around the perimeter of the cell ready to torment me.... They were the color of pitch-black. They were pure evil and looked like professional executioners and torturers.... They were full of self-satisfaction because another soul was entering their domain. Some demons held instruments with which to torture and inflict unimaginable pain on me.... I would have to suffer through endless torture.[16]

Her friend called a pastor at the church to pray for her since she was in torment, and when he prayed:

...the demon's claw that gripped my head was pried loose, and my spirit being was immediately sucked back into my body....After the shock of what happened wore off, when I was broken and alone, I finally repented to the Lord....After I repented, I felt the intense grip of Satan leave me for good.[17]

With all she experienced, it changed her life. She is now a Christian, at peace, and living for God. My wife and I have met her, and we feel she is a very kind, genuine, and sincere woman.

Rebecca Springer was close to death, and one day she had a vision of heaven. She writes:

I was...resting upon the softest and most beautiful turf of grass, thickly studded with fragrant flowers....I observed how perfect each plant and flower was....Beneath the trees, in many happy groups, little children were laughing and playing....I saw...elegant and beautiful houses of strangely attractive architecture....There was no shadow of dust, no taint of decay on fruit or flower. Everything was perfect.[18]

She also was so privileged to meet Jesus. As she states:

With a low cry of joy and adoration, I threw myself at His feet....I hung upon His words, I drank in every tone of His voice....And I was exalted, uplifted, and up-borne, beyond the power of words to express.[19]

## A Dream of Perry Stone

Perry Stone writes of another dream he had in 2009:

I was walking with my beloved father, Fred Stone. In the dream Dad had become quite feeble, walking with a cane....I assisted him into a large building....I stood watching him move down the hall, when suddenly something came rising up out of the floor. Dad stopped, and I saw it was a large weight scale—the kind a person would stand upon to weigh themselves....It gently lifted Dad from the floor about twelve inches. As he stood there, a most remarkable metamorphosis occurred. Dad's gray hair began to change to the original coal black that he had in his twenties. His stooped shoulders went straight...he looked the way he did in his late twenties....Dad had been "weighed" for his life's work and ministry and was found worthy to enter this heavenly paradise. I suddenly observed a room...at that moment my beloved grandfather John Bava peeped around the corner to see where Dad was! I then realized there was a waiting room full of people who Dad had personally known throughout his life and had already passed on who were awaiting his arrival.[20]

Perry saw much more, but the point is that we will be with our families in heaven, the ones who know Jesus as their personal Savior. The Bible states that when the patriarchs died they "gave up the ghost" and were "gathered to [their] people" (Gen. 25:8; 35:29).

Another vision told by Pearl Ballew Jenkins states:

An angel who was my guide...showed me the beauties of Heaven and the horrors of Hell...the Golden City...the splendor of it surpassed anything I had ever beheld....Surrounding the City were great groves of palms and many other tropical plants...green grass...a river....On its banks were evergreen trees whose leaves glistened like diamonds...fountains of sparkling water.[21]

She went on to say:

> I...saw many people dressed in white robes....There was a long table, around which they were gathered. Jesus was standing at the head of it, serving them as they came in....There was no noise, nor discord, but soft, sweet strains of music filled the place with melody, and all was in perfect harmony. It was Heaven![22]

She went on to say that she was then shown hell.

> I was carried down through darkness....Flames of fire were rolling over the heads of thousands of people....They were screaming, crying and calling for water, but no water was given. There was no relief from their torment and misery....The angel said..."This was Hell, and it is deep, deep, deep."...I felt an inexpressible urge to warn people not to go to that awful place....The heat of the flames is intense. There is no peace nor joy here. All is misery. It is eternal death. There is no end to it.[23]

Dr. Richard Eby, who had died and was shown heaven, also was later given a vision of hell. This is his story:

> In the twinkling of an eye Jesus was standing beside me...."My son...You must be able to tell them they can choose heaven or hell, but tell them that I died to close hell and open heaven just for them. They must choose between My love and eternal life, or Satan's lies and eternal death."...Instantly I realized I was a

dead sinner being taken to the lowest bowels of the earth....A sense of absolute terror gripped my being. The immensity of my isolation in the stark darkness and soundless silence was overwhelming....In the depths of the earth my isolation was terrifying. No one could help but Jesus, and He was gone!...I would never see another person; I could not break out; I would never hear a voice again— either friend or enemy. Nothing to read. Nothing to look at. Nowhere to go....I heard demons taunt me....And the smell! Horrid, nasty, stale, fetid, rotten, evil...stinking, crawling, demons seen mentally delighting in making me wretched....I would now have an eternity of inescapable nausea, beside all the rest of hell. My terror mounted until I was ready to collapse into utter hopelessness, crushing despair, abysmal loneliness. I was an eternally lost soul by my own choosing....The clammy wet walls held me crushed for eternity without escape, without a Savior, without anything to maintain sanity! And then it was over. The light flicked on....My wife...told me that I was not with it the rest of the day. She was quite right.[24]

Kenneth E. Hagin had a vision in which he was shown a glimpse of heaven and hell (Sheol). He states:

It seemed as if I went with Him through the air until we came to a beautiful city....Its beauty was beyond words....We came back down out of heaven, and when we got to earth we didn't stop, but kept going....We went down to hell, and as we went into that place I saw what appeared to be human beings wrapped in flames....Jesus told me, "Warn men and women about this place," and I cried out with tears that I would.[25]

Jesus told him:

> I speak and say, "Go speak to this one or pray for that one," but My people are too busy. They put it off and souls are lost because they will not obey Me.[26]

If you choose to reject the Word of God, and all these people's experiences, and the thousands more who have also had experiences like these, then it is your choice. When you stand before God, you will have no excuse. You will have sent yourself to hell by your own words, by your rejection of Jesus Christ (Matt. 12:37; Rev. 21:8).

# 8

# Do You Believe in an Afterlife?

YOU MIGHT SAY, "I don't believe in an afterlife." If that's the case, then you have to ask yourself these questions: if there is no heaven or hell, then there are no consequences for our actions, and no justice ever served. Would that be fair, especially for the murderers, the rapists, the child abusers, and the Hitlers of the world? In addition, there would be no rewards for those who sacrifice. Would that be just? And if there is a heaven, then are we simply entitled to go to this perfect place?

Why do many of the religions of the world believe in a heaven and a hell? I am not saying that all religions believe the same way, but there is a belief in the afterlife by most. The Old Testament writers, along with Jesus and the apostles, believed in an afterlife. They believed one would spend eternity either in paradise or in torment. Jesus said in Matthew 25:46: "And these shall go away into everlasting punishment: but the righteous into life eternal." There are many verses similar to these. (See Isaiah 33:12–14; Daniel 12:2; Matthew 7:13–14; 13:41–42, 49; 18:8; Mark 3:29; 9:43; 16:16; John 5:29; 15:6; Acts 24:15; 2 Thessalonians 1:9; Revelation 14:10–11; 20:13–15; 21:8.)

Dr. Erwin W. Lutzer writes, "The writers of the Old Testament believed that to go to sheol was not only to go to the grave but also to experience a conscious afterlife."[1]

83

Perry Stone writes, "Angels are literal, demons are literal, and heaven and hell are literal....Any attempt to make hell a nonliteral place is futile, humanistic unbelief. Any effort to teach that the fire is spiritual and not literal also has no place in the true interpretation of the complete revelation of hell in both Testaments...The departed souls of men and women who have died in Christ are now in heaven in paradise."[2]

The great evangelist Billy Graham points out, "Centuries before Christ, the Babylonians believed in 'The Land of No-Return.' The Hebrews wrote about going down to the realm of Sheol, or the place of corruption; the Greeks spoke of the 'Unseen Land.' Classical Buddhism recognizes seven 'hot hells,' and the Hindu Rig Veda speaks of the deep abyss reserved for false men and faithless women. Islam recognizes seven hells. Jesus specifically states that nonbelievers will not be able to escape the condemnation of hell (Matthew 23:33)....The Bible teaches there is hell for every person who willingly and knowingly rejects Christ as Lord and Savior."[3]

Again, Billy Graham states, "Jesus mentions Heaven about seventy times in the book of Matthew alone....The Bible teaches us that our bodies are flesh and bone, and they will die eventually—but that we also are immortal, eternal souls. The soul (or spirit)...will never die, but will live forever in either Heaven or Hell."[4]

Jesus mentioned the word *heaven*, or a derivative of it one hundred twenty-five times in the New Testament. Jesus also mentioned the word *hell* fifteen times. Eleven times the word *hell* is the Greek word *Gehenna*, which is a word Jesus used to describe what hell would be like. There are also forty-six verses in which Jesus mentioned hell, a place of destruction, torment, and everlasting fire. Other writers of the New Testament used the word *hell* eight times. This was clearly a warning that hell is a literal place.

Randy Alcorn states, "After Christ returns, there will be a

resurrection of believers for eternal life in Heaven and a resurrection of unbelievers for eternal existence in Hell (John
5:28–29)."[5]

Wayne Grudem says, "Scripture frequently affirms the
fact that there will be a great final judgment of believers
and unbelievers. They will stand before the judgment seat
of Christ in resurrected bodies and hear his proclamation of
their eternal destiny."[6]

Walter Martin states, "Death is not extinction, and hell is
not an illusion—everlasting conscious punishment is a terrifying reality of God's infinite justice upon the souls of unbelieving men."[7]

In Acts 17:30–31 Paul states, "God…now commandeth
all men every where to repent: Because he hath appointed
a day, in the which he will judge the world in righteousness
by that man whom he hath ordained; whereof he hath given
assurance unto all men, in that he hath raised him from the
dead." (See also Matthew 25:31–33; John 5:26–27; Acts 10:42;
Romans 1:18; 2 Timothy 4:1; Revelation 20:12.)

Every person will stand before God and be judged (Rev.
20:12–15).

## What Will Heaven Be Like?

Some people have great misconceptions in regard to what
heaven will be like. The devil has deceived people into
thinking that heaven is a boring place. Some think it is
going to be an eternity of only singing hymns. John Eldredge
writes, "Nearly every Christian I have spoken with has some
idea that eternity is an unending church service.…We have
settled on an image of the never-ending sing-along in the
sky, one great hymn after another."[8]

Heaven will be the most exciting and active place, far
beyond what our minds can imagine. We will enjoy eternal
life with Jesus, family, and loved ones (Gen. 15:15; 37:35; 49:33;

2 Sam. 12:22–23). We will be forever learning about God and His Word (Ps. 119:89, 93, 160; Matt. 24:35). There are great books of knowledge to read (Josh. 10:13; 2 Sam 1:18; 1 Kings 11:41; 1 Chron. 29:29; 2 Chron. 9:29; 12:15; 20:34; Ps. 56:8; Isa. 34:16; Jer. 32:12; Mal. 3:16-18; Rev. 20:12). In describing what heaven will be like, Randy Alcorn says, "There are also other books in Heaven…"[9] He goes on to give scripture referring to books in heaven such as Psalm 56:8, Malachai 3:16-18, and Revelation 5:1, 5; 20:12. We will be learning for all eternity, but without the limitations imposed by our weak flesh. We will sing the praises of God and be in awe of God's presence (Rev. 22:4).

One of the things some of us will be doing is ruling over cities. Jesus said to the man He gave a pound to invest with, since he gained ten pounds, "Because thou hast been faithful in a very little, have thou authority over ten cities" (Luke 19:17). Some will be ruling over nations (Rev. 2:26). Since there are cities, there will be many events and activities taking place, as any city would have. In Matthew 25:23 Jesus said to the men He gave two talents and five talents, "Well done, good and faithful servant; thou hast been faithful over a few things, I will make thee ruler over many things: enter thou into the joy of thy lord." In Matthew 18:4 Jesus states, "Whosoever therefore shall humble himself as this little child, the same is greatest in the kingdom of heaven." Jesus also said in Matthew 5:19, "Whosoever therefore shall break one of these least commandments, and shall teach men so, he shall be called the least in the kingdom of heaven: but whosoever shall do and teach them, the same shall be called great in the kingdom of heaven."

There will be different rewards in heaven. Some will have a great reward in the kingdom (Matt. 5:12; 6:18; 11:11; Mark 9:41). Jesus said in Matthew 23:11, "But he that is greatest among you shall be your servant." (See Matthew 20:27;

24:46.) Jesus said He came to serve, not be served. In Luke 22:27 Jesus said, "But I am among you as he that serveth." To be great in God's kingdom we must learn to be a servant.

There will be precious things to enjoy and an inheritance reserved for us (Deut. 33:13; Ps. 37:18; 1 Pet. 1:4). There will be treasure stored up for those who are not concerned about storing up treasure on earth (Matt. 6:19–21). Jesus stated that He is preparing a mansion for each one of us (John 14:2). I'm sure we will be astonished by the architecture. We know there are windows, doors, walls, stories, and pillars in heaven (2 Kings 7:2; Ps. 78:23; Amos 9:6; Job 26:11; Rev. 21:11–23). There is every precious stone in abundance, where even the walls are made of all manner of rare stones (Rev. 21:19). Heaven will far exceed our wildest dreams. First Corinthians 2:9 says, "Eye hath not seen, nor ear heard, neither hath entered into the heart of man, the things which God hath prepared for them that love Him."

There are streets of pure gold, so pure that they look transparent (Rev. 21:18, 21), and there are beautiful trees (Rev. 2:7; 22:2) and food to eat (Ps. 78:25; Isa. 25:6; Matt. 26:29; Luke 14:15–24; 22:18, 29–30; 24:41; Rev. 2:7; 19:9). There will be a banquet prepared for us (Song of Sol. 2:4; Isa. 25:6; Luke 22:29–30). We will have a body like Jesus had after His resurrection, of flesh and bone. He ate after His resurrection (Luke 24:39; 1 John 3:2). He had His glorified body, as we will also have. We can sleep if we so desire (Ps. 127:2). There will be interesting forms of travel. Elijah was picked up in a fiery chariot (2 Kings 2:11; Ps. 68:17; 104:3; Isa. 66:15; Hab. 3:8). The speed of travel will be faster than light, since heaven is reached in a second (Ps. 11:4; Eccles. 5:2; Acts 7:49; 2 Cor. 5:8). There is a beautiful sea of glass (Rev. 4:6). There will be singing (1 Chron. 25:7; Ps. 104:33; Isa. 38:20; Mark 14:26; Eph. 5:19; James 5:13; Rev. 5:9; 14:2–3, 15:2–3) and instruments to play (1 Chron. 25:1–8; Ps. 150; Isa. 38:20; Rev. 8:7–13; 15:2). We will be able to pet a lion (Isa. 65:25). There will be amazing angels with all their power, immense size, and strength to behold (Ps. 103:20; 2 Pet. 2:11). The angels are an innumerable army (Dan. 4:35; Jer. 33:22). There will be no sickness in heaven and no pain (Rev. 21:4). There will be no more death or loss of loved ones (1 Cor. 15:55; Rev. 21:4).

We will be able to sit down with great leaders of the past who were Christians. We will talk with Adam and Eve, Noah, Abraham, Moses, King David, King Solomon, Daniel, Joseph, Isaiah, Jeremiah, Ezekiel, Esther, Paul, all the apostles, and more (Matt. 26:29; Luke 13:28–29). Above all, we will be able to see Jesus and talk with Him (Matt. 26:29; Rev. 22:4). We will be able to inquire of God in His temple (Ps. 27:4). Can you imagine learning from God Himself the answers to the many questions and interests we all have?

The Bible even describes a new city that descends out of heaven and comes to the earth. It is placed on a new, refurbished earth (Isa. 65:17; 66:22; 2 Pet. 3:13; Rev. 21:1–2, 10). This new city is where most Christians will dwell. Revelation 21:1–2 tells us, "And I saw a new heaven and a new earth.... And I John saw the holy city, new Jerusalem, coming down from God out of heaven from God, prepared as a bride adorned for her husband."

Randy Alcorn says:

> According to the prophets, the apostle Peter, and Christ himself, our destiny is to live forever on a restored and renewed Earth.... Scripture describes Heaven as both a country (Luke 19:12; Heb. 11:14–16) and a city (Heb. 12:22; 13:14; Rev. 21:2). Fifteen times in Revelation 21 and 22 the place God and his people will live together is called a city. The repetition of the word and the detailed description of the architecture, walls, streets, and other features of the

city suggest that the term *city* isn't merely a figure of speech but a literal geographical location.... The city at the center of the future Heaven is called the New Jerusalem.... It is perched on the peak of a hill.[10]

Dr. Erwin W. Lutzer states:

> Let's consider some features of this beautiful permanent home. The dimensions are given as a cube, fifteen hundred miles square. "And the city is laid out as a square, and its length is as great as its width; and he measured the city with a rod, fifteen hundred miles; its length and width and height are equal" (Rev. 21:16). If we take that literally, heaven will be composed of 396,000 stories (at twenty feet per story) each having an area as big as one half the size of the United States!... John wrote in the Revelation that the city had the glory of God. "Her brilliance was like a very costly stone, as a stone of crystal-clear jasper" (21:11).... The new Jerusalem is a city of unimaginable beauty and brilliance.[11]

Abraham was looking forward to dwelling in this city. Hebrews 11:10 states: "For he looked for a city which hath foundations, whose builder and maker is God."

Philippians 3:20 says: "We are citizens of the state...which is in heaven" (AMP; see also Luke 10:20; John 14:2; 2 Cor. 5:1; 1 Pet. 1:4; Rev. 22:14). There will be other cities on the earth also (Luke 19:17–19). Life will be similar, as we will have our family and friends, providing they were Christians.

Perry Stone writes, "Heaven itself is very much like Earth, with rivers (Rev. 22:1), trees (v. 2), a city (Rev. 21:2), mountains (Heb. 12:22), books (Rev. 20:12), and so many other things."[12]

It is a place I am certainly looking forward to, and I will be privileged to live there with my beautiful wife forever.

## Three Very Important Verses About Heaven

Scripture contains 740 verses about heaven; here are 3 of the most important:

> » Matthew 7:21: "Not every one that saith unto me, Lord, Lord, shall enter into the kingdom of heaven."

> » Matthew 18:3: "Verily I say unto you, Except ye be converted, and become as little children, ye shall not enter into the kingdom of heaven."

> » John 14:2: Jesus Himself said, "In my Father's house are many mansions: if it were not so, I would have told you. I go to prepare a place for you." He promises to prepare a place for us (1 John 2:25).

## Are We Too Comfortable?

There are those who are preoccupied with their own comfortable lives, and they are not looking forward to the boring life they've imagined in heaven. Heaven does not sound so inviting to some. Of course, they are misinformed. In our country we have been very blessed and have been able to enjoy many wonderful things. Some can feel too comfortable to actually look forward to heaven.

Edward Donnelly writes:

> For the most part, we are comparatively rich, reasonably healthy, tolerably happy. Life is sweet and, without realizing it, we are drugged by well-being

and prosperity....We have traded "the sweet by and by" for the prosperous here and now....Society offers us a dazzling range of experiences, from the new technologies of interactive entertainment to ever more exotic foreign holidays. The very comfort of this world makes heaven less inviting.[13]

It is like one author wrote:

If you were offered a handful of $1,000 bills or a glass of cool water, which would you choose? The $1,000 bills, of course—*anyone in his right mind would.* However, if you were crawling through a desert, dying of thirst...which would you take? The water, of course—*anyone in his right mind would.* That's called "circumstantial priorities." Your priorities change according to your circumstances....At the moment, you may not be interested in the offer [salvation, heaven], but on Judgment Day your circumstances will radically change. Then it will be too late.[14]

We must come to the realization that after we leave this blessed life, we will not be able to enjoy anything good at all unless we dwell in heaven, because "Every good gift and every perfect gift is from above, and cometh down from the Father of lights" (James 1:17). Unless we know Jesus personally, we will never experience "good" after this life.

We are able to enjoy the good in life because Psalm 33:5 says, "...the earth is full of the goodness of the LORD." However, after we die, we can only experience His comforts and blessings in heaven, because they don't exist anywhere else. Since our souls are eternal (Gen. 1:26), we will live forever in one of two places: heaven or hell. Hell was prepared for the devil and not for man. Man has a choice. Since heaven and God are perfect, He cannot let us in to heaven the way we are. We would corrupt it just as we have the earth. Revelation 21:27 states, "And there shall in no wise enter into it any thing that defileth, neither whatsoever worketh abomination, or maketh a lie: but they which are written in the Lamb's book of life." We have to be given a new heart and a new spirit to enter heaven, and that cannot come through good works (2 Cor. 5:17; Eph. 2:8–9; Titus 3:5). It can only come through a relationship with Jesus Christ (John 14:6).

God is a three-part being.

First John 5:7 says, "For there are three that bear record in heaven, the Father, the Word, and the Holy Ghost: and these three are one." (See also Genesis 1:26; Matthew 28:19; Mark 1:10–11; John 14:26, 16:13; 1 John 4:14.) There are at least fifty-four other verses in the New Testament in regard to the Trinity.

Man is a three-part being. First Thessalonians 5:23 tells us: "…and I pray God your whole spirit and soul and body be preserved blameless unto the coming of our Lord Jesus Christ." (See also Genesis 2:7; 35:18; 1 Samuel 25:29; 1 Kings 17:22; Job 32:8; 33:28; Psalms 26:9; 34:22; 49:8–9; 116:8; 141:8; Proverbs 20:27; 23:14; Ecclesiastes 3:20–21; 12:7; Isaiah 26:9; 38:17; Matthew 10:28; Luke 12:5; Acts 7:59; 2 Corinthians 4:16; James 2:26.)

Perry Stone writes: "One reason that the afterlife is 'everlasting' is that all humans consist of three parts—'spirit, soul, and body' (1 Thess. 5:23). The body returns to dust; however, the human spirit is eternal and cannot be destroyed or annihilated."[15]

My question for you is: Do you know where your soul will go after you die?

# 9

# God Doesn't Give Up!

THESE ARE SOME personal stories we experienced and were greatly impacted by.

## Unexpected Tragedy

I had just finished speaking at a church in the San Diego area, and the pastor's grandson, Mike (not actually his real name), shared with me about his best friend (we will call him Nick), who was twenty-three years old. He said he'd brought his friend to hear me speak, but his friend said he didn't believe in God, heaven, hell, or anything else I spoke about. Mike said to him, "You are my best friend, and I want you to go to heaven with me." The atheist, Nick, said, "Don't talk to me about that Bible junk; I am not interested." Well, a couple of weeks later they were having breakfast together, and Mike tried to share with Nick again about God. Nick again said, "Don't ever talk to me again about this nonsense. I am not going to become a Christian, so leave me alone." Mike was sad, but he honored his friend's request and stopped trying to convince him at the breakfast. Nick got up from the table, got in his car, and drove off. Five minutes later he was in an automobile accident and hit a brick wall. He died instantly. This is a true story.

Mike was so upset he'd lost his best friend, but he was much more upset because, unless Nick had changed in those last few minutes, he would be in hell. How horrid, because he didn't have to go there. It was his stubborn will, the fact that he wouldn't listen, that would have brought about that fate. His friend had spoken to him many other times, and so did others. We all have a free will. God won't force anyone into heaven.

## Given a Last Chance!

There was another time when I had an appointment to list a home for sale in the neighborhood where I had been selling them. Toward the end of the appointment the woman began telling me about her battle with cancer. It was obvious she was not well. As a matter of fact, I felt like she might not make it through the appointment, she looked that bad. I felt so sorry for her. I asked her if I could pray for her. She quickly responded with a strong "No!" I asked her why, and she said she didn't believe in God, that the Bible was all fairy tale stories. I tried my best to explain to her about how much God loves her and His desire is for her to go to heaven. She again mocked me and refused to listen. I kept attempting to reach her, as I felt inside she wouldn't be around much longer. No matter what I said, no matter how much I explained the love of God, she wouldn't listen, and she actually started to get angry with me. So I got up from the table and told her I would begin the marketing of her home as she'd asked. Well, the next morning she was dead.

Now I couldn't help thinking that if she didn't think about what I had told her, and she didn't repent and call out to Jesus, then I knew where she would be for all eternity. She would now have an eternity in hell to think about her foolish decision. God had tried to get through to her, even to the last day, but she'd refused to listen.

You see, people are not in hell because they didn't know. They know, but they refuse to accept God's free gift. Why would anyone refuse such a wonderful gift? It is simply illogical. It is because it is spiritual. The devil blinds people, but they are the ones who entertain the devil's lies. Jesus said in Matthew 13:15, "For this people's heart is waxed gross, and their ears are dull of hearing, and their eyes they have they closed." Notice, *they* close their own eyes. They don't want to see it or hear it, just like the elderly woman whom I pleaded with to listen. She said she didn't believe in God. Jesus said that our own words will condemn us (Matt. 12:37).

Billy Graham states, "Will a loving God send a man to hell? The answer from Jesus and the teachings of the Bible is, clearly, 'Yes!' He does not send man willingly, but man condemns himself to eternal hell because in his blindness, stubbornness, egotism, and love of sinful pleasure, he refuses God's way of salvation and the hope of eternal life with Him."[1]

One other point is, you don't know that you might be the last person whom someone meets that day before they die. If we share the Word of God, we may change someone's eternal destiny. We must be careful to obey God and preach the gospel.

## An Eternal Perspective

There was a twelve-year-old girl who came up to my wife and me after we had just finished speaking. We were in the back of the church meeting people. She came up to us in tears. She told us that a year earlier someone had given her our book, and she read it and immediately asked Jesus into her heart. She had become a Christian, but her entire family was not. She said she began praying for them to get saved and had continued praying for one year. The following year, she had heard that my wife and I would be speaking at a church in her hometown. She was so excited and wanted to meet us. She begged her family to come to hear us speak. To her amazement, they agreed to come—the entire family of brothers and sisters, parents and grandparents. She was weeping because they had all gone forward in the altar call and had given their hearts to the Lord. Then she said, "Here they all are; I want you to meet my entire family." They were all crying and so happy.

The main point is this: we were so impressed with this young girl because she had an eternal perspective to be so concerned about her family at such a young age. She wouldn't let go of our hands as she continued to laugh and cry in excitement. We will never forget her, and I think about it: What if we had not gone on that trip? We need to be obedient to do whatever the Lord instructs us to do. My wife and I sometimes do not want to get up so early, drive to Los Angeles, fly across the country, change our planes, rent a car, drive another two hours, stay in another hotel room, listen to the neighboring room play their TV all night, and so forth. It's not easy to go on all these trips, but the results encourage us to continue.

## What Twenty-Five Cents Will Buy!

Another time after I finished speaking and inviting people to come forward to commit their lives to the Lord, a seven-year-old boy came up to the stage and was crying. He said he had just come forward in the altar call and had given his heart to Jesus. He wanted to thank me for showing him the way and setting him on the right course. He then reached into his pocket and said, "I want to give you this, to support your ministry because you changed my life. I know you will change others too! This is all the money I have." And he handed me a quarter. I was so touched. Imagine: only seven years old and already having the maturity to be concerned for others and to give all he had! We were so honored. I took the time to encourage him and thank him for his support, and most of all, for his commitment to serve God. We have placed the quarter in a frame and will keep it always. There are many fifty-year-old Christians who do not have the concern and insight for others that he showed. As the Bible says: "Out of the mouth of babes..." (Ps. 8:2). His quarter earned him a lot of respect with me and an open hand from God.

## Too Tough for God to Reach?

Another encounter I will share is with my neighbor. He was a tough, old, stiff-necked guy who was not at all interested in God. I liked him, though, as he was direct and didn't pull any punches. However, he would not even allow a conversation about God. Well, one day we found out he was in the hospital dying of cancer. His wife said that he had almost died the night before and was barely hanging on. We asked if we could go and visit him. She said, "Of course, but don't bring up religion. He won't have it." We went that day, and after we had talked a bit, he shared with us that he had almost died the night before. He said he could feel himself slipping out of his body and that he was terrified for the first time in his life. For this man to be scared was quite something, because he was a war hero, tough and strong, and the unemotional type. We asked him what he was so afraid of. He explained that he had felt total darkness and terror. He said, "I have never been so afraid, and I don't know where I was going, but I knew it wasn't a good place."

We explained to him that the reason he was afraid was because he was headed for a place he really didn't want to end up. We told him that the Bible speaks of such a place, a place of unimaginable horror. We also told him that God loved him and wanted to take him to heaven. However, what he needed to do was to make a decision. He would need to understand his need for a Savior, ask forgiveness for his sins, and accept Jesus Christ into his heart. We took some time and explained salvation to him, and after a while, he grabbed our hands and, with a tear coming down his face, asked if we would lead him in a prayer to accept Jesus into his heart. We prayed with him, and he told us he suddenly felt a total peace come over him. He said it was a peace that he had never felt before. He was so happy and thanked us profusely. We visited a while and then assured him of his eternal home in heaven. We left, and the very next day he passed on. Again, we were so glad we had gone to see him.

It is amazing that many people will not even talk about God until they are on their deathbeds. The problem is that many will not have the opportunity to be on their death-beds to accept Jesus. They could be killed suddenly. Proverbs 29:1 says, "He, that being often reproved hardeneth his neck, shall suddenly be destroyed, and that without remedy." (See also Proverbs 6:15; 24:22; Isaiah 29:5; 47:11; 1 Thessalonians 5:3.) This man got a taste of the afterlife beforehand, and then he changed. You may not be so fortunate!

## Stubborn but Submissive

There was a thirteen-year-old girl who approached me after I finished the altar call at a church where I was speaking. She told me that about a year ago one of her friends gave her a book she should read called *23 Minutes in Hell*. Well, she threw it in the trash. About a week later, another girl-friend told her she should read a book called *23 Minutes in Hell*. She still didn't read it. Then, a few weeks later, a third girlfriend gave her our book and told her she must read it. She still didn't read it. This went on for another month, where everyone she knew was giving her our book, unaware of the others. She said she thought it was very strange. She began counting all the people who had told her to read the book, and the total was twenty-three people in all at the end of a month! That really got her attention, since it was the number twenty-three. She finally decided to read it, and she accepted the Lord and said the prayer at the end of our book. She just wanted to thank me, and she said that the number twenty-three had special meaning to her now, and she was so grateful to be a Christian. The biblical meaning of the number twenty-three is "death." She finally decided to die to herself and to live for God.

The main point I want you to see is how many times the Lord tried to get through to her. God was persistent, sending twenty-three people to her to get her attention. If she had not told me this story herself, I wouldn't have believed it. God doesn't give up. It's our own stubborn will that rejects Him for the final time, and then He allows us to go our own way.

## Down to the Wire!

There was a man (we will call him John) with whom I served on the board of our homeowners association. He was dying of a disease. He was a very intelligent and educated man, and a man I appreciated to have with me on this board. He was gruff and had no patience and no tolerance for foolishness. He just wasn't a social person, and most people didn't like him. But he sure knew the rules and regulations for the neighborhood! Well, I had always befriended him over the years, and he knew I appreciated his intelligence. Even though he was an atheist, we got along very well. I never preached to him, and I thanked him often for his knowledge and contribution to the neighborhood.

One day he ended up in the hospital, and this time it was very serious. He was seventy-five years old and in very poor health, dying of a deadly disease. He was down to about one hundred pounds. I knew he had no friends, and his family was deceased, except for one brother. I found out he had been in the hospital for a week. I felt strongly compelled to go see him this one day. When I arrived, I discovered the doctors hadn't expected him to have made it through the night, and he was barely hanging on. I was glad I came. I began to talk with him (he could barely whisper), and I told him again how much I appreciated his vast knowledge about so many things. But I shared this with him: "John, even though you have learned so much in life and have experienced so many things, there is one subject I believe you have never investigated. This one subject I have dedicated much of my life to investigating and living out. So, would you mind if I share what I know about this with you?" He said, "No, I don't mind, and I am anxious to hear about what I already know you will share."

He knew my lifestyle, but I had never preached to him before. I began to explain to him that he was getting ready to embark on a journey that would last for all eternity. In addition, I told him that he was not prepared for what lay ahead. I explained salvation, what it meant to be a Christian. I said there were only two destinations that you face, and it is your choice which one you will spend eternity in. If you don't ask God to forgive you of your sins and invite Jesus into your heart, you will not spend your eternity in heaven but in hell. I told him that God was calling out to him now, and no one could come to God unless He called them (John 6:37, 44). "Now is your time," I explained. I shared some stories out of the Bible and answered his questions. After two hours, he asked, with tears in his eyes, if he could accept the Lord as his Savior. I gladly led him through a prayer, and he understood what he was doing. He cried and cried, and thanked me for showing him the way. He was never open to hearing about the Bible before, but now he knew he would not make it through the night. Well, later that evening, he did pass away. I was sorry to hear that he had gone, but I was also so very happy that he made it to heaven and that I had obeyed that still, small voice telling me to go and see him that day.

The main point I want you to see is this: Look at God's

long-suffering (Rom. 2:4; 1 Tim. 1:16; 2 Pet. 3:15). Even though this man had vehemently denied Jesus his entire life, God still was trying to get through to him even at the last minute. Even if someone curses and hates God, God will still accept him into heaven if he repents. Look at the thief on the cross (Luke 23:43). God always tries to wake people up to the truth, even to their last breath.

> » Psalm 86:5 says: "For thou, Lord, art good, and ready to forgive; and plenteous in mercy unto all them that call upon thee."

> » Psalm 145:8–9 says: "The LORD is gracious, and full of compassion; slow to anger, and of great mercy. The LORD is good to all: and his tender mercies are over all his works."

And the second point is this: when God tells us to go visit someone and share our faith, we should be careful to obey immediately. The question I pose for you is this: Would God hold me accountable if I hadn't gone to see him? Before you answer, you might want to look at these verses and commentary opinions:

> » Ezekiel 33:8 says: "If thou dost not speak to warn the wicked from his way, that wicked man shall die in his iniquity; but his blood will I require at thine hand."

> » Acts 18:6 says: "Your blood be upon your own heads; I am clean."

> » Acts 20:26 says: "I am pure from the blood of all men."

> » Acts 20:27 says: "For I have not shunned to declare unto you all the counsel of God."

» Colossians 1:27–28 says: "Christ in you, the hope of glory: whom we preach, warning every man."

If we shun in this respect to declare all the counsel of God, part at least of the responsibility of their ruin will lie at our door.[2]

It is a solemn responsibility, and we do harm to our own soul if we do not fulfill it faithfully.[3]

Certainly the consequence for such unfaithfulness on the preacher's part includes divine chastening and loss of eternal reward (cf. 1 Corinthians 4:1–5).[4]

The blood of those who perish through their carelessness *will be required at their hand.* It shall be charged upon them in the day of account that it was owing to their unfaithfulness that such and such precious souls perished in sin; for who knows but if they had had fair warning given them they might have fled in time *from the wrath to come?*[5]

You will be accounted by Me as a manslayer, held accountable in the realm of works (not salvation) and suffer reward or loss of reward as the case may be…personal responsibility.[6]

God is not saying we are expected to witness to every person we see. However, we are to be careful to obey God when He directs us to a *certain individual.* If we don't obey, I believe Scripture is clear that God will hold us partially accountable. We will not lose our salvation, but we will lose our reward and feel shame on that day. In His mercy He will wipe away every tear, and that is what some of our tears will be caused from (Rev. 21:4). It is a very sobering thought that we will be held accountable, and we should take it seriously. Our job is to be a witness of Jesus Christ (Mark 16:15). Now, most of our witness is through our life example, but also we should seek every opportunity to share the Word of God with others. It is a wonderful privilege to be entrusted with the gospel, but it is also a very serious responsibility.

First Thessalonians 2:4 tells us: "But as we were allowed of God to be put in trust with the gospel, even so we speak; not as pleasing men, but God, which trieth our hearts."

## A Mother's Persistence

I will share one more story, and this one is very personal. My younger brother died of cancer just recently. Losing an immediate family member is a very heart-wrenching matter to endure, as you may know. We all miss him very much. He was a kind person, he had a good heart, and he would do anything for you. He was a hard worker, and he cared greatly for his four children. He had been divorced many years back, which was extremely difficult for him to handle, mainly because of his children. One day he lost his job in the economic slump. He was a roofer, which is very hard work, especially in Florida where it gets extremely hot in the summer. He was now only getting the really poor jobs that nobody wanted, but he would take them just to make some income. He had always been a respected roofer in the industry, and he was known for his excellent work. He had the ability to do the most difficult roofs that many others couldn't. It was sad to see him have to take such lowly jobs, with all his talent. He was also getting too old to continue doing such hard work, since he was fifty-three. He had some very serious injuries, broken bones and the like, and the doctor told him not to work any longer. But he was determined to give as much as possible to his family. His children were the pride of his life. However, he was in a lot of pain now, and it was getting almost impossible to do the work. He normally would come home from a hard day on the roof, and he would find relaxation in a few cigarettes and a couple of beers. However, as it became even more difficult to find work, he began getting depressed, and he started drinking and smoking more and more. He was now in a lot of debt, and he couldn't earn nearly enough to keep up with it all. He also had his car repossessed. His credit was ruined. There were bills everywhere. This went on for years. He'd had to give up his place years earlier, and he had to move back in with our parents. He had many disagreements with our dad, which just added to the stress he already had.

My wife and I would talk to him about Jesus over the years. He respected us, and he loved us very much, but he wasn't interested in God or in giving up his lifestyle. He also wasn't willing to give up smoking and drinking. He had done both since he was a teen, but now he had gotten much worse. He was up to two to three packs per day and a dozen beers every night. We tried to convince him to quit, but he didn't think it would hurt him. We would encourage him often, and we told him we really respected how much he loved his children. We told him we respected how hard he would work, and how no job was too low for him to have to take. We were proud of him, and we knew Jesus would help him get out of the mess he was in if he would commit his life to Him. We spent hours explaining just what he could do, but he took none of our advice. We continued to pray for him, even to help him financially at times.

Well, one day he found out he had cancer of the liver, lungs, and throat. We prayed for him every day, and we met with him to explain that God could deliver him from that disease, if he would change and trust Him. After forty years of my mother praying for him, he did finally confess a prayer with us accepting Jesus into his heart, but he still wasn't willing to change his lifestyle. I believe he truly acknowl-edged Jesus as the Savior and Son of God, and he believed that He died for our sins. He mentally assented to this fact, but it was not a heartfelt acceptance of Jesus. He did not make Him Lord over his life. He was not willing to repent (Matt. 4:17; Luke 13:3; Acts 17:30), which is a willingness to walk away from a sinful lifestyle (John 5:14, 8:11). My brother wasn't willing to make a commitment to live for God. He wasn't interested in going to church, or reading the Bible, or finding new Christian friends, or getting to know God in any way. He also would not even consider giving up his beer and his cigarettes, or his cursing, or the occasional promis-cuous encounters with women. We told him that God would help him change and give him the grace and strength to quit, but he was unwilling. He didn't think it was wrong, and he didn't think it would kill him.

As a quick side trail, in regard to seeing what true repen-tance is like, look at the story of Zacchaeus. He was a rich tax collector, hated by the people. He was considered a sinner, as tax collectors would gouge the people, taking more than what was required by the government. Zacchaeus had climbed up a tree to be able to see Jesus in a crowd of people following Him. Jesus saw him and told him He wanted to stay at his house that night. The people criticized Jesus for wanting to stay at such a sinner's house (Luke 19:5-7). During the evening, "Zacchaeus stood, and said unto the Lord: Behold, Lord, the half of my goods I give to the poor; and if I have taken any thing from any man by false accusation, I restore him fourfold" (v. 8).

My point is this: when Zacchaeus was convicted in his heart, he immediately repented and gave back what he had stolen. He didn't have to struggle with giving up tax col-lecting or returning what he had taken illegally. Jesus said, "This day is salvation come to this house..." (v. 9). This man got saved, and his repentance, which was reflected in his returning the stolen money, was proof of it. If someone truly repents, then it is in their heart to do right. My brother showed no interest in any change of lifestyle, as Zacchaeus did. Psalm 55:19 says, "Because they have *no changes*, therefore they fear not God" (emphasis added).

My mother, who is truly a saint if there ever was one, had been faithful to pray for my brother every day and many hours a day for over forty years. She stayed with him in the hospital around the clock for weeks before he died. During the last two to three months, he was in absolute agony, and pain medication no longer worked. It was so difficult to see him in such severe pain, and it was especially hard on my mother. Twelve years prior Annette and I had pleaded with him to give up his addictions, but even then he refused to listen.

The last two days he went into a coma. In the coma, he suddenly sat up in the bed, cried out, and said, "Thank You, Jesus. Thank You, Jesus." Then he lay down and died.

God, by a miracle, had him speak out of a coma in order to let our mother know that he had finally cried out to Jesus. He must have seen Jesus and known Jesus loved him and was taking him to heaven. God is so merciful, to save him at the last minute. He would have saved him long ago, if Tommy would have cried out and submitted to Him. Even though he had confessed the prayer (Rom. 10:9–10), there was no repentance. And without repentance, there can be no forgiveness (Matt. 3:2; 4:17; Mark 1:14–15; 6:12; Luke 13:3; Acts 3:19; 17:30; 26:20; Rev. 2:16). Repentance is a requirement for salvation. Only God knows if he would have gone to heaven earlier, but Scripture is clear regarding a repenting heart.

My mom wouldn't give up, and neither did Jesus. We are so grateful for God's mercy and goodness. I miss my brother very much, but I am so thankful that I will see him again in heaven. It was so hard to see him suffer from the pain of the cancer and to have had such difficulties in life. He didn't need to go through all of that, but his lifestyle was his choice. God instructs us how to stay healthy, and He tells us how He will provide for us. It is through our obedience to His Word (Josh. 1:8; 2 Chron. 26:5; Prov. 3:9–10; 22:4; 28:27; Isa. 48:17; 1 John 3:22).

Every one of us must repent and receive Jesus as our Lord and Savior. It has nothing to do with how good we are. It is based on our relationship with Him (John 11:25–26; Acts 4:12). Good works should follow our commitment to the Lord, but good works won't save us. God will give everyone every last possible opportunity to repent and receive His Son as their Lord and Savior. He is merciful and longsuffering, as the Bible states! It is we who are stubborn and resistant to His Word.

# 10

# The "Dead" Could Tell Us a Thing or Two!

THERE ARE THOUSANDS who have had these near-death experiences or who even have died and have then come back to life. However, most people will be skeptical of such an experience, and that is understandable. Even Abraham said to the rich man in hell, "If they hear not Moses and the prophets, neither will they be persuaded, though one rose from the dead" (Luke 16:31). Even if someone said they came back from heaven or hell, most people would simply think they were crazy. As a matter of fact, Jesus Himself rose from the dead, and so many don't believe that established fact. However, Jesus was dead for three days. The stone was rolled away with the guards there. They would never have let that happen willingly, as their own heads would have been chopped off. After His resurrection, Jesus was seen by over five hundred people, and even secular historians wrote about it. He was physically touched by several people. His resurrection is very well documented, so it is evident that He rose as He said He would.

I have met and talked to many who have had an experience with seeing heaven or hell, who have no reason to lie, who are reputable, honest people. Most have not written a book, and only some are sharing their experiences. Most do not share their experiences so as to avoid ridicule. As I have said, it is not important for us to believe anyone's experience.

The only thing that *is* important for us to believe is what God's Word states!

There are three people listed in the Bible who came back and spoke to people after they had died: the prophet Samuel, Moses, and Elijah. However, all of God's people expected to see their loved ones in heaven after they died. There are also a few who got a peek at the afterlife. These next verses show us that we can expect a life after death.

> » Genesis 15:15: God, speaking to Abraham, said, "And thou shalt go to thy fathers in peace; thou shalt be buried in a good old age." God believes we exist after death and that we will be reunited with the ones in our family who knew Him.

> » Genesis 37:35: "For I will go down into the grave [sheol] unto my son mourning." Jacob expected to see his son again after he died. Sheol is the Hebrew word meaning "the realm of the dead."[1] The *Vine's Expository Dictionary* states that: "Sheol...never denotes the grave...Sheol wrongly rendered the grave."[2]

> » Genesis 49:33: "And when Jacob had made an end of commanding his sons, he gathered up his feet into the bed, and yielded up the ghost, and was gathered unto his people."

> » 1 Samuel 28:14: King Saul heard the voice of the prophet Samuel as the prophet spoke to him and told him what was to take place the next day. Many of the commentaries, such as the *Believer's Bible Commentary*, believe it was actually Samuel. I agree for these reasons: Verse 15 says, "And Samuel said to Saul..." The Bible would not have identified him as Samuel (also

in verse 20) if it was an evil spirit. It would have accurately recorded it as an "evil spirit" if that were the case. Also, Samuel foretold exactly what would take place the following day: that Saul and his sons would be with him that following day, and that Israel would be defeated and delivered into the hands of the Philistines. Samuel pointed out to the king that the Lord had taken the kingdom out of his hands and given it to David, because of Saul's disobedience to the Lord and for not executing God's fierce wrath on Amelek (1 Sam. 15:2–3, 9, 28, 35; 28:14–20). Why would a lying spirit now speak all this truth and chastise Saul for not killing an evil king, and how could an evil spirit correctly predict the future? In addition, the witch was startled and cried out, not really expecting it to be Samuel. Since she recognized it to be Samuel, she then knew it was King Saul, because most knew that the prophet was usually with the king. She described Samuel as with a mantle. "Mantle, or robe, the habit of a judge which Samuel had sometimes worn…"[3] It seems clear through the chapter it was actually Samuel. He was still alive and well in Paradise.

» 2 Samuel 12:22–23: "I shall go to him, but he shall not return to me." David wept over his child who died, and stated he would go to be with him. He obviously expected to see him when he died. He believed in an afterlife, as he stated in many verses throughout the Bible.

» 2 Kings 2:11–12: "There appeared a chariot of fire, and horses of fire, and parted them both asunder; and Elijah went up by a whirlwind into heaven. And Elisha saw it..."

» Job 3:11, 13: "Why died I not from the womb?...For now should I have lain still and been quiet, I should have slept." He stated he would still exist and be in a better place than his current suffering if he had died at birth.

» Isaiah 14:9–10: "Hell from beneath is moved for thee to meet thee at thy coming...and they shall speak and say unto thee, Art thou also become weak as we?" Obviously they still exist to be able to speak! (There are no atheists in hell.)

» Ezekiel 32:21–31: "The strong among the mighty shall speak to him out of the midst of hell...Asshur is there and all her company: his graves are about him...yet have they borne their shame with them that go down to the pit. They have set her a bed in the midst of the slain...her graves are round about him...which are gone down to hell...their iniquities shall be upon their bones...all of them...and bear their shame with them that go down to the pit. Pharaoh shall see them." As you can see, they must still exist to be round about each other, and have a bed, and bear shame, and their iniquities, and be seen by Pharaoh.

» Jonah 2:2: "Out of the belly of hell [sheol] cried I, and thou heardest my voice." Many commentaries believe Jonah was at the gates, or just inside the gates of sheol, so obviously he still existed.[4]

» Matthew 17:2: Jesus had a conversation with Moses and Elijah (Mark 9:4). They had died hundreds of years earlier. Obviously they still existed.

» Luke 16:23–31: "And in hell he lift up his eyes, being in torments [severe pain, torture], and seeth Abraham afar off, and Lazarus in his bosom. And he cried and said…but Abraham said…" They both spoke to each other, so obviously those who are in heaven and hell still exist.

» John 12:9–11: "And they came not for Jesus' sake only, but that they might see Lazarus also, whom he had raised from the dead. But the chief priests consulted that they might put Lazarus also to death; because that by reason of him many of the Jews went away, and believed on Jesus." Lazarus was able to testify firsthand that life existed after death. The Sadducees didn't believe in the resurrection of the dead.

» Acts 7:59: When Stephen was about to die from being stoned, he cried out and said, "Lord Jesus, receive my spirit." In verse 55, Stephen "looked up stedfastly into heaven, and saw the glory of God, and Jesus standing on the right hand of God."

» 2 Corinthians 12:4: Paul was "caught up into paradise, and heard unspeakable words…"

» Revelation 4:1: John was told to "come up hither," into heaven in the spirit, and was shown things in heaven and things to come. He was escorted by and conversed with an angel (Rev. 22:8–10).

» Revelation 5:13: John states, "And every creature which is in heaven, and on the earth, and under the earth, and such as are in the sea, and all that are in them, heard I saying, Blessing, and honour, and glory, and power, be unto him that sitteth upon the throne, and unto the Lamb for ever and ever." John points out that there are people under the earth and in heaven who speak.

» Revelation 6:9–10: "And when he had opened the fifth seal, I saw under the altar the souls of them that were slain for the word of God…and they cried with a loud voice, saying…" They were alive after death and cried out, and also they were in heaven.

» Revelation 20:13–15: "And death and hell delivered up the dead which were in them: and they were judged every man according to their works." Again, it is apparent that people still exist, as there were people in hell, and they were all judged.

» Revelation 22:8–9: "And I John saw these things, and heard them [things in heaven]. And when I had heard and seen, I fell down to worship before the feet of the angel which shewed me these things. Then saith he unto me…" (John was in heaven talking with an angel.)

» Luke 13:3: [Jesus said:] "I tell you, Nay: but, except ye repent, ye shall all likewise perish." We have to turn from our sins and ask for forgiveness. Jesus said He was the only way of salvation (John 14:6). He has spoken to us before and after He had risen from the dead. He also said in John 11:25–26, "I am the resurrection, and the life: he that believeth in me, though he were dead, yet shall he live: And whosoever liveth and believeth in me shall never die."

# 11

# What Religions Tell Us

THERE ARE MANY religions in our world, but if I can ask, what has any of their leaders done for you? Has any one of them dealt with the sin issue? Has any one of them died for your sins and risen from the dead—except for Jesus? In this chapter we will look at a brief overview of the beliefs of some of these religions. In the following pages I will list some of the unique attributes of Christianity in comparison.

Perry Stone points out, "Religion is formed for men to reach up to God (or a god), but redemption is God reaching down to man. Anyone can form a religion, establish a belief, and make certain laws and regulations for their followers, but these activities have nothing to do with redeeming a human soul from hell. People do not spend eternity in hell because they are Hindu, Jewish, or Muslim, but they do so because they have no redemptive salvation covenant that delivers them from the eternal death penalty."[1]

Man has to be redeemed, because we are all born in sin (Rom. 5:12; Eph. 1:7).

Romans 6:23 states: "For the wages of sin is death; but the gift of God is eternal life through Jesus Christ our Lord." No other religion explains our sin problem so succinctly.

In addition, Perry states: "It is interesting that all major world religions have a belief in some form of the afterlife, and even a belief in some form of hell. This belief goes all the way back to the ancient Egyptians and can be found in the Hindu, Buddhist, Islamic, Jewish, and Christian religions."[2]

Billy Graham has stated, "Most of the world religions are based upon philosophical thought, except for Judaism, Buddhism, Islam, and Christianity. These four are based upon personalities. Only Christianity claims resurrection for its founder. Abraham, the father of Judaism, died about nineteen centuries before Christ. There are no evidences for his resurrection. Buddha lived about five centuries before Christ, and taught principles of brotherly love. It is believed that he died at the age of eighty. There are no evidences for his resurrection. Muhammad died AD 632, and his tomb at Medina is visited by thousands of devout Mohammedans. His birthplace at Mecca sees many pilgrims each year. However, there are no evidences for his resurrection."[3]

Billy Graham went on to describe some of the religious beliefs of those he has encountered throughout the world. He states: "In China when my wife was growing up, frequently babies who died before cutting their teeth were thrown out to be eaten by pariah dogs. The people feared that if evil spirits thought they cared too much for the children they would come and take another one. They tried to prove their indifference in this crude way....I once saw a man in India lying on a bed of spikes. He had been there for many days, eating no food and drinking little water. He was attempting to atone for his sins. Another time in Africa I saw a man walk on coals of fire. Supposedly, if he came through unscathed, he was accepted by God, if he was burned, he was considered to be a sinner in need of more repentance. In India, a missionary who passed the banks of the Ganges noticed a mother sitting by the riverbank with two of her children. On her lap was a beautiful new baby and whimpering beside her was a painfully retarded child of about three. On her return home that night, the missionary saw the young mother still sitting on the riverbank, but the baby was gone.... Horrified at what she thought might be true, the missionary... asked her what had happened... the mother looked up and said, 'I don't know about the god in your country, but the god in mine demands the best.' She had given her baby to the god of the Ganges. People have made human sacrifices in the name of religion.... In the name of religion, kings, emperors, and leaders of nations and tribes have been worshiped as gods.... An example of the class of monarchs worshiped as deity was the Mikado, the spiritual emperor of Japan. In an official decree he received the title of 'manifest or incarnate deity.'"[4]

John Ankerberg and John Weldon list the following highlights of other religions[5]:

> » *"Christian Science*, founded by spiritist Mary Baker Eddy, teaches that, 'there is no death.'... To Christian Scientists 'heaven and hell are states of thought, not places.'"

> » *"Edgar Cayce*, a spiritist and New Age prophet, said that 'the destiny of the soul, as of all creation, is to become One with the Creator' and that no soul is ever lost.'"

> » "New Age cult leader and spiritist Sun Myung Moon, of *The Unification Church*, believes that 'God will not desert any person eternally. By some means... they will be restored.'"

> » *"Mormonism*, founded by occultist Joseph Smith, argues, 'The false doctrine that the punishment to be visited upon erring souls is endless... is but a dogma of unauthorized and erring sectaries, at once unscriptural, unreasonable, and revolting.'"

» *"Jehovah's Witnesses*, founded by Charles Taze Russell, maintains that the wicked are forever annihilated because 'The teaching about a fiery hell…can rightly be designated as a "teaching of demons."'"

» *"The church of the New Jerusalem* (Swedenborgianism), founded by spiritist Emanuel Swedenborg, emphasizes that God 'does not condemn anyone to hell.'"

» *"Eckankar*, a New Age religion founded by spiritists Paul Twitchell and Darwin Gross, insists that 'there is no death'…and that there is no eternal hell."

» *"Lucis Trust* and The Arcane School/Full Moon Meditation Groups, begun by New Age spiritist Alice Bailey, argue that 'the fear of death is based upon…old erroneous teaching as to heaven and hell.'"

» *"The Love Family* (The Children of God), founded by spiritist David Berg, views hell as a temporal purgatory: 'the lake of fire is where the wicked go to get purged from their sins—to let them eventually come…out.'"

» *"Rosierucianism*, an occult philosophy, declares that 'the "eternal damnation" of those who are not "saved" does not mean destruction nor endless torture,'…and that 'the Christian religion did not originally contain any dogmas about Hell…'"

» *"Unitarian Universalism* confesses the following: 'It seems safe to say that no Unitarian

Universalist believes in a resurrection of the body, a literal heaven or hell, or any kind of eternal punishment.'"

» "*The Theosophical Society,* founded by medium Helena P. Blavatsky, declares: 'we positively refuse to accept the...belief in eternal reward or eternal punishment...' Hence, 'Death...is not...a cause for fear.'"

» "Ramtha, the spirit speaking through medium J. Z. Knight, claims, 'God has never judged you or anyone,' and 'No, there is no Hell and there is no devil.' 'Lilly' and other spirits channeled through medium Ruth Montgomery argue that 'there is no such thing as death' and that 'God punishes no man.'"

## Scientology

Dr. Walter Martin points out:

Scientology teaches that the Bible is a byproduct of Hindu scriptures.

God or gods may exist, but the individual must decide for himself.

Christ is a legend that preexisted earth-life on other planets and was implanted into humans on earth. Jesus was just a shade above "clear" and was no greater than Buddha or Moses.

Reincarnation sufficiently explains man's existence, but Scientology is the freedom from reincarnation.

Man is basically good and in his evolution, he will finally become a godlike being known as "homo novis."

The Church of Scientology is the most litigious religion in the history of churches founded in the United States.... The founder of Scientology, Lafayette Ronald Hubbard... a popular science fiction writer of the 1930s and 1940s, changed venues midstream by allegedly announcing at a New Jersey science fiction convention, "Writing for a penny a word is ridiculous. If a man really wants to make a million dollars, the best way is to start his own religion."... His later cynicism of Christianity betrays his virtually faithless upbringing....

Several competent writers have gathered contradictory evidence of Hubbard's exaggerated vita and have challenged his claims. None are so thoroughly damaging to his credentials than Russell Miller's *Bare-Faced Messiah: The True Story of L. Ron Hubbard* and former Scientologist Bent Corydon's *L. Ron Hubbard: Messiah or Madman.* Miller showed that Hubbard attended high school in America while he was claiming to have been traveling in Asia. His medical records showed that he was never crippled, blinded, or wounded in World War II, let alone being pronounced dead twice. (All this he claimed.) Bent Corydon, formerly head of one of the most successful Scientology missions (Riverside, California), has countless court transcripts, affidavits, and firsthand testimonies that lay many of L. Ron Hubbard's claims to rest.

Hubbard's academic degrees have come under question, since Sequoia University was discovered to be an unrecognized diploma mill located in a two-story house in Los Angeles. It was closed down in 1958 by an act of the California Legislature.[6]

The rest of the story regarding this religion just gets worse and worse. It would be extremely beneficial for anyone involved in this belief to read Dr. Martin's book, as he has documented all the facts in such a thorough way.

## Unification Church

Sun Myung Moon claimed he was a messiah. He wrote a book entitled *The Divine Principle*. In his own book, Dr. Walter Martin states: "*The Divine Principle* is authoritative scripture in the Unification Church and is considered superior to the Bible....Devastating to the credibility of Moon's supposed vision is that every Unification writing gives the date as 'April 17, 1936, Easter morning.' The gravest error in Unification history occurs here. Our calculations prove beyond a doubt that Moon's vision could not have occurred on Easter morning, because April 17, 1936 was a Friday, not a Sunday....One of the most astounding confessions by Moon himself was under oath in 1982, during a Unification suit against a deprogrammer. Moon, in a New York Federal Court testimony, on May 27 and 28, stated that he had met Jesus, whom he had recognized from 'holy cards.' He also testified that he had met Moses and Buddha."[7]

This self-proclaimed messiah died on September 3, 2012. Not such a divine messiah!

## Unitarianism

Fritz Ridenour states that, "Unitarians do not believe that people are sinners. They believe that man should not look to God for help, but should be his own savior...all that is required is to live a good life and follow the Golden

Rule…They do not believe there is a heaven or a hell, and there is no need of salvation through Jesus Christ. The very idea of hell is an insult.

Ridenour goes on to mention the similarities between Unitarianism and humanism: "Because so much unitarian thinking puts man above God, it was only natural for unitarianism to become linked to secular humanism, which became popular during the twentieth century with publication of The Humanist Manifesto I and The Humanist Manifesto II. Among the many points made in these manifestos are claims that there is no God and that the universe has always existed."[9]

I like what Randy Alcorn wrote about what we will say when we get to heaven in regard to man's being "good": "We'll never question God's justice, wondering how he could send good people to Hell. Rather, we'll be overwhelmed with his grace, marveling at what he did to send bad people to Heaven. (We will no longer have any illusion that fallen people are good without Christ)."[10]

## Buddhism

In looking at Buddhism, Fritz Ridenour states, "The man who formulated Buddhism was Siddhartha Gautama, who was born a Hindu about 560 B.C. at Lumbini near the border of India in what is now Nepal.…One of Buddha's most important teachings was his theory of the middle way…a spiritual path of salvation…which have come to be called the 'Four Noble Truths':

> » "Suffering is universal…
>
> » "The cause of suffering is craving (selfish desire)…
>
> » "The cure for suffering…is to eliminate craving…

» "Suppress craving by following the Middle Way—the Noble Eightfold Path. First, Buddha isolated the cause, tanha—humanity's inability to escape from the squirrel cage of death and rebirth. Next he worked out a system called the Eightfold Path by which a Buddhist could rid himself of tanha.

"Buddha claimed that whoever could follow [the] Eightfold path would eventually reach nirvana, a release from the endless cycle of death and rebirth. The three main kinds are Hinayana, Mahayana and Tantrism. Hinayana means, 'the doctrine of the lesser way,' referring to the belief that... only a fortunate few lifelong monks can find nirvana.... Mahayana Buddhism, the doctrine of the 'greater way' teaches...the idea of savior gods...Buddha...[stayed] to save mankind and became the first and supreme [savior god]...who can be called on by the faithful...Tantric Buddhism uses incantations and occult signs...that can leave its followers open to demonic activity...Buddha said that, 'to live is to suffer'...that suffering comes from craving—desire or attachment of any kind. Buddha taught that the only way to rid oneself of selfish desire was through self-effort....For a person to master himself, he must have a higher source of strength.... [Buddha] ignored the possibility of help from God...to overcome these desires."[11]

Dr. Walter Martin also writes a detailed chapter on Buddhism, but he sums it up with these comments: "Classical Buddhism maintains that cycles of rebirths are necessary in order to attain Nirvana....God is not a person...They behold God when they behold themselves."[12]

## Hinduism

Josh McDowell states, "*Moksha*, also known as *mukti*, is the Hindu term used for the liberation of the soul from the wheel of karma. For the Hindu, the chief aim of the existence is to be freed from *samsara* (the binding life-cycle) and the wheel of karma with its endless cycles of births, deaths and rebirths. When one achieves this liberation, he enters into a state of fullness or completion. . . . In Hinduism, one's present state of existence is determined by his performance in previous lifetimes. . . . As one performs righteous acts, he moves toward liberation from the cycle of successive births and deaths. Contrariwise, if one's deeds are evil, he will move further from liberation. The determining factor is one's karma. The cycle of births, deaths and rebirths could be endless. *Samsara* refers to transmigration or rebirth. It is the passing through a succession of lives based upon the direct reward or penalty of one's karma. This continuous chain consists of suffering from the results of acts of ignorance or sin in past lives. At each successive rebirth, the soul, which the Hindus consider to be eternal, moves from one body to another and carries with it the karma from its previous existence. The rebirth may be to a higher form, i.e., a member of a higher caste or god, or down the social ladder to a lower caste or animal, since the wheel of karma applies to both man and animals. . . . On the subject of God, Hinduism's being is the undefinable, impersonal Brahman, a philosophical absolute. . . . In Hinduism there is no sin against a Holy God."[13]

Dr. Maurice S. Rawlings, who has investigated thousands of near-death experiences and those who have had visions of heaven or hell, says this: "Interestingly, none of the deathbed visions I have encountered suggest that reincarnation would occur—that they would return to earth as a newborn or would inhabit another person already born."[14]

## Christian Science

Dr. Walter Martin has, again, a detailed chapter on this topic, but here are some highlights:

- » "God is divine principle.
- » "Jesus is not God. The incarnation and bodily resurrection of Jesus Christ did not occur.
- » "Scripture is not inerrant.
- » "Sin, death, and evil do not exist.
- » "There is no literal, physical existence of the material universe.
- » "Mary Baker Eddy—'Mother' and Leader, the 'Discoverer and Founder' of Christian Science."[15]

She showed some of her mental condition when her third husband, Asa, died "of a coronary thrombosis....She contested the autopsy report, and the physician she chose confirmed her conviction that Asa died of 'arsenic poisoning mentally administered.' Such a radical report prompted an inquiry into the credentials of Mrs. Eddy's physician, Dr. C. J. Eastman....It was found that 'Dr.' Eastman was running a virtual abortion mill, and had no medical credentials whatever to justify his title. He was sentenced to ten years in prison....Mrs. Eddy's letter to the *Boston Post* dated June 5, 1882, in which she accused some of her former students of mentally poisoning Asa Eddy with malicious mesmerism in the form of arsenic mentally administered is one of the most pathetic examples of Mrs. Eddy's mental state ever recorded and one which the Christian Science Church would like to forget she ever wrote."[16]

Some of her beliefs are documented in Dr. Walter Martin's book as follows: "From Eddy's *Science and Health*, the textbook of the 'Christian Science' she claimed to discover in 1866... 'Disease being a belief, a latent delusion of mortal mind... all disease is cured by the mind.... What is God? Jehovah is not a person. God is a principle.... Matter is mortal error...' From Eddy's *Science and Health with Key to the Scriptures*... 'There is no life, truth, intelligence nor substance in matter. All is Infinite Mind and its infinite manifestation, for God is all in all.... There is no physical science, the principle of science is God, intelligence and not matter, therefore, science is spiritual for God is Spirit.... He has no personality, for this would imply Intelligence in matter; the body of God is the idea given of Him in the harmonious universe...'" To further point out, Dr. Martin proves that she plagiarized much of her supposed what "God Almighty spoke" from P. P. Quimby, considered the father of Christian Science. He is the one who even came up with the name "Christian Science" and used it "for some time before Mrs. Eddy gratuitously appropriated the terminology as her own, something she dared not do while the old gentleman was alive and her relationship to him known to all."[17]

There is much more proof documented in Dr. Martin's book that will open your eyes to the truth behind this false religious belief.

## Jehovah's Witnesses

Josh McDowell states: "The Jehovah's Witnesses are a product of the life work of Charles Taze Russell, born February 16, 1852.... Their theology denies every cardinal belief of historic Christianity including the Trinity, the divinity of Jesus Christ, His bodily resurrection, salvation by grace through faith, and eternal punishment of the wicked.... *The Watchtower* makes it clear they do not believe in the doctrine of the

Trinity....The Trinity doctrine was not conceived by Jesus or the early Christians....Jesus, the Christ, a created individual...He was a god, but not the Almighty God, who is Jehovah....The truth of the matter is that the word is Christ Jesus, who did have a beginning."[18]

As you can see, their beliefs completely conflict with the Bible and mainstream Christianity.

## Mormonism

Joseph Smith, Jr., the founder of Mormonism....In 1820, Joseph allegedly received a vision that became the basis for the founding of the Mormon Church...."My object in going to enquire of the Lord was to know which of all the sects was right, that I might know which to join...the personages who stood above me in the light...I was answered I must join none of them, for they were all wrong."...The Mormon Church has four accepted sacred works: the Bible, the *Book of Mormon*, *Doctrine and Covenants*, and *The Pearl of Great Price*....The *Book of Mormon* is also considered inspired....The Mormons believe in many gods and teach that God himself was once a man. Moreover, Mormon males have the possibility of attaining godhood. Joseph Smith made this clear in *The King Follett Discourse*: "God was once as we are, and is an exalted man....We have imagined and supposed that God was God from all eternity. I will refute that idea...he was once a man like us...you have got to learn how to be Gods yourselves...the same as all Gods have done before you."[19]

It's amazing that so many would believe that for 1,800 years since Christ, all the church fathers were deceived and missed

God. Some of the greatest theologians and intellects to ever live over all those years were all wrong, but this one fifteen-year-old was right! How foolish can one be! Also, Jesus said in Matthew 16:18: "The gates of hell will not prevail against it" (the church). I guess we are supposed to believe that Jesus missed it too since He said His church would not be prevailed against!

The pamphlet *Mormonism, What You Need to Know* tells us:

> The Mormon Church teaches, "The head God called together the God's [*sic*] and sat in grand council to bring forth the world.... The Father has a body of flesh and bones as tangible as man's.... The appointment of Jesus to be the Savior of the world was contested by one of the other sons of God—Lucifer. This spirit-brother of Jesus desperately tried to become the Savior of mankind."[20]

Josh McDowell and Dr. Martin have written very thorough chapters on this religion also. My book is not meant to cover all the religions or even to go into any significant detail, but only to give you some highlights. If you read Dr. Martin's book and some other credible sources, you will see that most of the founders of other religions also have, at the very least, dubious and sinister backgrounds and, of course, they disagree with the Bible.

As you can see, just about all the religions of the world have been founded by one individual, by one man's vision or idea. In the above-mentioned religion, the founder claims he had a visit from God Himself. Well, first off, that's an obvious clue that he was deceived. The Bible states that no man has ever seen God the Father (1 John 4:12), yet he said he had. So right from the start, he is in error. Second, God would never come to one person to tell him He was not happy with the entire church. Jesus said, "My sheep hear my voice" (John

10:27). God speaks to all of His church, not just one person. He especially doesn't speak about His church to someone who is not in His family, who is not His child; then if that person writes his beliefs, which are contrary to the Bible, he is obviously not God's child (John 1:12, 8:44, 17:9; Rom. 9:7–8; Gal. 3:26; Eph. 1:5; 5:1). Thinking you are the only one who has been told by God Himself that all the church is wrong is extreme pride, extreme deception, or extreme ignorance. In addition, if God were to do something as foolish as that, why would God have waited from the time of Jesus until the year 1850, when Joseph had his visit, to tell him He was not happy with His church? Why would He have waited so long, and then why would God have trusted a fifteen-year-old with this most important message? The Mormon beliefs contradict the Bible in so many areas, as Josh McDowell and Dr. Martin point out in their books. It also contradicts the Bible in the area of having three additional books. The Bible clearly tells us not to add or to take away anything from the Bible (Deut. 4:2; 12:32; Prov. 30:6; Rev. 22:18–19). We are not to have additional books to live by—and they have three! Dr. Martin does an excellent job documenting all the facts in regard to this false religious belief in his book *The Kingdom of the Cults*. The Bible teaches clearly that Jesus is God, He created all things, was born of a virgin, became a man, lived a sinless life, suffered and died for our sins on a cross, shed His blood, rose from the dead, saved us from an eternal hell, ascended into heaven, and will take those who believe in Him to heaven (Mark 1:10–11; 14:62; Luke 22:70; John 1:1; 3:16, 36; 6:40; 8:24; 9:37; 10:30, 36; 11:25; 12:47; 14:6; 16:13; Acts 3:19; 4:12; 17:30; Rom. 3:10–12, 23; 5:8–9; 6:23; 10:9–10; 1 Cor. 15:3–4; Col. 1:16–17; Heb. 1:2; 1 John 1:7–9; 4:14; 5:11; 5:7).

Most of the religions of the world provide no assurance of going to heaven. They are all based on works. Perry Stone again states: "I have asked some Muslims if they have an assurance of going to heaven, and they do not. Only if they follow the Quran, pray, give to charity, follow the five pillars of Islam, and make *hajj* in Arabia, *then* they may be found worthy. Even Orthodox Jews follow laws, regulations, rituals, and customs in an attempt to make it into the kingdom of heaven."[21]

If you are going to put your eternal soul in the trust of one of these beliefs, you would owe it to yourself to read some of these books first to know the facts. Then you can make an informed decision. The bottom line is, what have their founders ever done for anyone? Have their founders died for sins and risen from the dead? Only Christianity can claim that. Some will state that Jesus was a good teacher or a morally good person. But they will not admit He was the Son of God, died for our sins, and rose from the dead, as He said He would. Jesus said He was the Son of God. So how could you call Him a morally good man if you don't believe His words? You would have to say He was a liar—or a lunatic! Christianity has a solid, proven foundation and a risen Savior who loves us. Every person must repent of their sins and receive Jesus as their Lord and Savior in order to be saved from hell and enter heaven. If you would rather believe in a religion that is based on only one man's vision with questionable character, disregard the Bible, and disregard all the documented people who saw heaven or hell, then you have that choice. But remember, you are gambling with your eternal soul. Are you really willing to throw the dice?

# 12

# Why Is Christianity Unique?

S O WHAT IS the difference in Christianity from all other religions? There are at least seven primary differences that make Christianity unique.

First, no other religious leader has risen from the dead, as Jesus said He would (Matt. 17:23; 20:19; Mark 9:3; 10:34; Luke 9:22; 13:32; 18:33; 24:46; John 2:19). And as Dr. Henry Morris and Martin E. Clark point out: "The empty tomb has never been explained, except by the bodily Resurrection. If the body actually were still there, or in any other place still accessible to the Jews or Romans, they would certainly have produced it as a sure means of immediately quenching the spreading flame of the Christian faith. If the Apostles or other friends of Jesus somehow had the body themselves, and thus knew He was dead, they could never have preached His Resurrection as they did, knowing it would surely mean persecution for them and possibly death. No man will willingly sacrifice his life for something he knows to be a lie!...Jesus Christ alone, of all men in history, has conquered man's greatest enemy—death. The founders of other religions are all dead and their tombs venerated. The tomb of Christ is empty, and His bodily Resurrection from the grave is the best proved fact of all history!"[1]

Dr. William Lane Craig states: "The historical reliability of the story of Jesus' burial supports the empty tomb....Second, even if the disciples had preached Jesus' resurrection despite his occupied tomb, scarcely anybody else would have believed them. One of the most remarkable facts about the early Christian belief in Jesus' resurrection was that it flourished in the very city where Jesus had been publicly crucified. So long as the people of Jerusalem thought that Jesus' body was in the tomb, few would have been prepared to believe such nonsense as that Jesus had been raised from the dead. And third, even if they had so believed, the Jewish authorities would have exposed the whole affair simply by pointing to Jesus' tomb or perhaps even exhuming the body as decisive proof that Jesus had not been raised."[2]

I list many more quotes from scholars in Appendix B, defending the empty tomb. There is no other religious leader who has ever risen from the dead: only Jesus Christ, the Son of God (Matt. 17:9; 20:19; 26:32; Mark 9:31; 10:34; 14:28, 62; Luke 18:33; 22:70; 24:7, 46; John 8:24; 9:35; 10:30, 36; 11:25; 14:6; Acts 17:3; Rom. 8:34; 1 Cor. 15:20; Col. 3:1).

Second, no other religion deals with the sin issue. Even though some might like to think their sin is not that bad, all sin has to be dealt with (Rom. 6:23). There is a law of sin and death (Rom. 8:2). We cannot expect to go through life, do as we please, and then have no consequences for our actions. We all would agree that the child abuser, the murderer, and the Hitlers of this world should see justice. Yet, when it comes to ourselves, we naturally think we are not all that bad. However, as I pointed out in chapter 2, not one of us is "good enough" to simply stroll into a perfect heaven (Job 15:16; Ps. 51:1–5; 143:2; Isa. 64:6; Gal. 3:22). Man's best is far short of God's idea of good. God's standard is perfect, and we are not (Rom. 3:10–12, 23). We all have need of a Savior. Jesus is the only one who came down from heaven, became a man, and lived a life free of sin. He took on the punishment for our sin, died in our place, and then rose from the dead (John 6:51; Acts 4:12; Rom. 5:15–18; 1 Cor. 15:3–4; 1 Tim. 1:15;

2:6). He dealt with our sin, washing it away with His shed blood (Rom. 5:9; 1 Cor. 11:25; Eph. 1:7; 2:13; Col. 1:14, 20; Heb. 9:12, 14, 22; 10:19; 1 John 1:7; Rev. 5:9; 12:11). If we don't repent of our sins, then our sin remains (John 9:41; Acts 22:16; Rev. 1:5). Also, only an eternal God can pay for our eternal sins, and only a sinless God can pay for sins by the shedding of His blood (2 Cor. 5:21; Heb. 9:22, 28; 10:12; 1 Pet. 2:22, 24; 1 John 2:2). The Bible says in Hebrews 9:22: "And without shedding of blood is no remission." Blood is the payment for sin, and it can only be shed by someone sinless (Rom. 5:9; Eph. 1:7; 2:13; Col. 1:14; Heb. 9:12, 14; 10:19; 1 Pet. 1:19; 1 John 1:7; Rev. 5:9). That someone is Jesus. He is the only man ever to live a sinless life (1 John 3:5). I am glad my sins are erased, forgiven, and forgotten (Ps. 103:11–12; Heb. 8:12; 10:17). What about yours?

Third, most religions are founded on one man's vision—one book, written by one man! Why should we believe this one man's vision? It could have been satanic in nature. The Bible isn't just one man's vision or even just one book. As Dr. Chuck Missler points out, "The collection of sixty-six books that we traditionally call *the Bible* even though penned by more than forty authors over a period of several thousand years..."[3]

"Written over a 1,500 year span; written over 40 generations; written by more than 40 authors, from every walk of life—including kings, peasants, philosophers, fishermen, poets, statesmen, scholars, etc....military generals...a prime minister...a doctor...a king...a tax collector...a rabbi... written in different places...written at different times... written on three continents: Asia, Africa and Europe, written in three languages....Finally, its subject matter includes hundreds of controversial topics. Yet, the biblical authors spoke with harmony and continuity from Genesis to Revelation. There is one unfolding story: God's redemption of man."[4]

All these men of the Bible wrote under the inspiration of the Holy Spirit (2 Tim. 3:16). All but one of the apostles were tortured and killed. Some of the other writers of the Old and New Testaments were also killed. If Jesus really hadn't risen from the dead, would all these apostles and others have suffered horrific deaths for something they knew was not true? Many died thirty or forty years after Jesus was resurrected and ascended into heaven. Would they really have died for a lie all those years later, along with literally millions over the centuries who have been killed by many evil leaders and dictators for their faith in Jesus Christ? I hardly think so!

All the authors of the Old Testament told about the coming Messiah. All the New Testament authors also wrote about Him, that He was crucified and rose from the dead (1 Cor. 15:3–4). There were no discrepancies or contradictions. (I cite some of the scholars who state the same in Appendix B.)

Fourth, the authors predicted the future with what could only be divine accuracy. There are over three hundred prophecies foretelling the coming Messiah. A prophecy is history written in advance. Only God is capable of foretelling the future. Isaiah 46:10 states: "I make known the end from the beginning" (NIV). Each author wrote something about Jesus. What other religious book foretells the future?

Josh McDowell states: "Wilber Smith, who compiled a personal library of 25,000 volumes, concludes that the Bible 'is the only volume ever produced by man, or a group of men, in which is to be found a large body of prophecies relating to individual nations, to Israel, to all the peoples of the earth, to certain cities, and to the coming of one who was to be the Messiah. The ancient world had many different devices for determining the future, known as divination, but not in the entire gamut of Greek and Latin literature, even though they used the words prophet and prophecy, can we find any real specific prophecy of a great historic event to come in the distant future, nor any prophecy of a Savior to arise from the human race."[5]

I have included in Appendix A thirty-eight of the three hundred verses in the Old Testament foretelling Christ's future, along with the fulfilled corresponding New Testament verses. This alone is proof that the future was told with accuracy, and only God could fulfill all those prophecies.

Fifth, most other religions teach that "works" are required in order for you to have any possibility of going to heaven. There are also no guarantees! The Bible teaches in Ephesians 2:8–9, "For by grace are ye saved through faith; and that not of yourselves: it is a gift of God: *not of works*, lest any man should boast" (emphasis added; see also Galatians 2:16; Titus 3:5). On the other hand, the Bible tells us clearly that we have full assurance of our salvation by trusting in Jesus Christ as our Lord and Savior and by repenting of our sins (Isa. 45:17; 51:6; Luke 13:3; John 3:36; 11:26; 14:6; Acts 17:31; Rom. 10:9–10; Heb. 5:9; 1 John 2:25; 5:11). We don't have to wonder or be afraid or doubt our salvation. We are promised and assured of it (Isa. 51:6; Acts 17:31; Heb. 5:9; 1 John 2:25). It is a free gift, and we cannot earn it.

Sixth, the Bible has been scrutinized by a vast array of scholars, historians, archaeologists, geologists, and the like for hundreds of years, and they have not found any discrepancies. Dr. John Warwick Montgomery states: "I myself have never encountered an alleged contradiction in the Bible which could not be cleared up by the use of the original languages of the Scriptures and/or by the use of accepted principles of literary and historical interpretation."[6]

"Bernard Ramm speaks of the accuracy: 'Jews preserved it as no other manuscript has ever been preserved…they kept tabs on every letter, syllable, word and paragraph. They had special classes of men within their culture whose sole duty was to preserve and transmit these documents with practically perfect fidelity—scribes, lawyers, massoretes…'"[7]

Josh McDowell continues: "H. L. Hastings, cited by John W. Lea…'If this book had not been the book of God, men would have destroyed it long ago.'"[8]

The Bible is also unique in that "it has been read by more people and published in more languages than any other book in history.… According to *The Cambridge History of the Bible*, 'No other book has known anything approaching this constant circulation.'"[9] Many have tried to destroy or outlaw the Bible, but it continues to flourish. Jesus said in Matthew 24:35: "But my words shall not pass away." (See also Psalm 119:89; Isaiah 40:8; John 10:35; 2 Timothy 3:16.)

Seventh, the Bible teaches of a God of love. No other religion speaks of their founder as one who loves us and gave his life for us (John 3:16; 6:40, 51; 1 Tim. 2:4–6; Heb. 2:9; 1 John 2:2). Most religions are based on a god who takes and demands sacrifices. Some even require child sacrifices, cutting, or suicide in the form of self-explosion. The Bible teaches us that our God is love (John 3:16; Rom. 5:8; 1 John 4:7, 10, 16).

Napoleon Bonaparte said, "I know men and I tell you that Jesus Christ is no mere man. Between Him and every other person in the world there is no possible term of comparison. Alexander, Caesar, Charlemagne, and I have founded empires. But on what did we rest the creation of our genius? Upon force. Jesus Christ founded His empire upon love; and at this hour millions of men would die for Him."[10] And millions have died for Him over the years, as many evil dictators have demanded Christians either renounce Him or be killed.

First Corinthians 13 explains just what love is. It reveals the characteristics of love. I would like to show you the opposite of what this scripture says in order to demonstrate my point. I will imply the negative in each characteristic.

First, "Love is not patient, it doesn't wait for anyone. Love is envious of everyone, love is puffed up, and stuck on itself only, love is embarrassing, love is selfish, is quickly angered, love always thinks the worst, rejoices in sin, and always thinks of evil. Love never wants the truth, will do nothing for nobody, doubts everything, has no hope, and won't ever last. Love always fails and never works." Well, you get the point. It's obvious what love is not!

The question is, do we reflect the God we serve in our lives? Will the world recognize us as Christians, the way the Lord said they should?

> » In John 13:34–35, Jesus said: "A new commandment I give unto you, That ye love one another; as I have loved you, that ye also love one another. By this shall all men know that ye are my disciples, if ye have love one to another."

> » First John 3:10 says: "Whosoever doeth not righteousness is not of God, neither he that loveth not his brother."

> » First John 2:9 states: "He that saith he is in the light, and hateth his brother, is in darkness even until now."

> » First John 4:7–11 tells us: "Beloved, let us love one another: for love is of God; and every one that loveth is born of God, and knoweth God.... God sent his only begotten Son into the world, that we might live through him. Herein is love, not that we loved God, but that he loved us, and sent his Son to be the propitiation for

our sins. Beloved, if God so loved us, we ought also to love one another."

Jesus clearly stated that our love toward others is how someone will recognize us as followers of Him. If we keep our eyes on Him, the love will show. We need to get our eyes off of ourselves and become more concerned for the needs of others. I like this quote from Henrietta Mears: "The man who keeps busy helping the man below him won't have time to envy the man above him."[11]

A great example of a person who truly demonstrates the love of God is the life of Arthur Blessitt. He is the man who has walked on every continent and island group, over forty thousand miles, carrying a cross. He is in the *Guinness Book of World Records* for the longest walk. He has led many thousands to accept the Lord as their Savior over those years, and he still does. He has endured incredible hardships in his travels. Besides the physical difficulty of carrying a huge cross through every continent and island group around the world, he was beaten, thrown in prison many times, left in the freezing cold, starved, stoned, spat on, had his life threatened, and many other horrid things. But in all of that he always was kind and loving to everyone, even to his enemies. Here is just a small sample mentioned in his book of what he experienced: "I faced a firing squad in Nicaragua; I was almost stoned and beaten in Morocco; I was attacked by police in Spain; a Los Angeles police officer tried to choke me in Hollywood; I survived an angry man's pistol attack in Orlando, Florida; a man in Birdseye, India, tried to burn the cross; and a man in Nigeria broke the cross."[12] His book is fascinating and reveals a true Christian's love for all, even in the midst of being abused and hated. Only the love of God in someone could cause a person to endure what this man has endured.

In addition Billy Graham has dedicated his life to saving souls. He has always been a humble and loving man, as so many would attest. He is an excellent example of a Christian, along with his son Franklin.

Some have asked me, "Bill, are you saying that a Christian is a better person than a non-Christian?" I like the answer given in *The Evidence Bible*, which states, "The Christian is no better than the non-Christian, but he is definitely better off. It is like two men on a plane. One is wearing a parachute and the other is not. One is not better than the other, but the man with the parachute on is certainly better off than the man who is not wearing a parachute. The difference will be seen when they jump. Jesus warned that if we 'jump' into death without Him, we would perish. Our great problem is a law that is even harsher than the law of gravity. It is the Law of an infinitely holy and just Creator. The Scripture warns us, 'It is a fearful thing to fall into the hands of the Living God.' They tell us we are His enemy. See Romans 5:10."[13]

I think that is a very clear picture of what it will be like to enter into eternity without God—without His parachute!

These next verses clearly show the love and patience of God toward us.

> » Jeremiah 3:12–13: "Come home to me again, for I am merciful.... Only acknowledge your guilt. Admit that you rebelled against the LORD your God" (NLT).

> » Jeremiah 5:1: "Run up and down every street...," says the LORD. "Look high and low; search throughout the city! If you can find even one just and honest person, I will not destroy the city" (NLT).

» Jeremiah 8:4–5: "When they discover they're on the wrong road, don't they turn back? Then why do these people stay on their self-destructive path? Why do the people…refuse to turn back [even though I warned them]?" (NLT).

» Jeremiah 25:4–9: "And the LORD hath sent unto you all his servants the prophets…but ye have not hearkened.…They said, Turn ye again every one from his evil way…and dwell in the land that the LORD hath given unto you.…Yet ye have not hearkened unto me, saith the LORD; that ye might provoke me to anger with the works of your hands to your own hurt."

» Jeremiah 26:3: "Perhaps they will listen and turn from their evil ways. Then I will change my mind about the disaster I am ready to pour out on them because of their sins" (NLT).

» Jeremiah 44:4–5: "Again and again I sent my servants, the prophets, to plead with them, 'Don't do these horrible things that I hate so much.' But my people would not listen or turn back from their wicked ways" (NLT).

» Lamentations 3:33: "For he does not enjoy hurting people or causing them sorrow" (NLT). The Lord has no pleasure in allowing punishment. The Lord over and over pleads for people to simply turn back to Him for He delights in showing mercy.

» Romans 2:4–5: "Don't you see how wonderfully kind, tolerant, and patient God is with you? Does this mean nothing to you? Can't you see that his kindness is intended to turn you from your sin?" (NLT).

You can see God's heart here! He clearly let the people know how to avoid evil, but they simply refused His instruction and goodness. May we learn through His Word, and not have to learn the hard way.

There are some who have the opposite problem. They have trouble loving themselves. As Pastor Gregory Dickow explains, "When we're lacking healthy love for ourselves, we feel inadequate, defective, and flawed.... Well, loving yourself—taking care of yourself, appreciating your special gifts, valuing yourself—is actually the first step toward loving anyone *else*. For if you don't love yourself, you are not a reservoir of love from which others can drink."[14]

Jesus summed up all the commandments in one statement found in Matthew 22:37–40: "Thou shalt love the Lord thy God with all thy heart, and with all thy soul, and with all thy mind. This is the first and great commandment. And the second is like unto it, thou shalt love thy neighbour as thyself. On these two commandments hang all the law and the prophets."

Remember, love never fails. That is an awesome promise. The test is, will we show love to the unlovely? This is how we separate other religions from Christianity. It is not simply by our lip service, but also by our actions. You will notice which churches and organizations are always at the disaster locations after a storm. It's the Christian churches and Christian organizations, like Samaritan's Purse and the like, who are present. Do we really love our brother if we do not help him? Jesus said in John 13:34–35: "A new commandment I give unto you, That ye love one another; as I have loved you, that ye also love one another. By this shall all men know that ye are my disciples, if ye have love one to another."

# 13

# What Does the Bible Say About Hell?

JESUS MENTIONED HELL, eternal damnation, eternal fire, everlasting punishment, outer darkness, and the weeping and gnashing of teeth in forty-six separate verses. He spoke of hell more than anyone else. Why did He mention it so much? Because that is what He saved us from! It was clearly a message of warning, and a message of warning is a message of love. What loving parent wouldn't warn their child not to play in a busy street? Several years ago when Hurricane Ike hit the Gulf Coast, the front page of a Texas newspaper read, "Certain Death to Those Who Don't Vacate." Now, you wouldn't say the writers of that article were being mean for issuing that statement, right? No, we would be grateful for the warning. In the same way, God is warning us about where we will end up if we do not repent of our sins and accept Jesus Christ as our Lord and Savior.

In Luke 16 Jesus made it very clear that a person still exists after death. Some say He was only speaking in a parable. However, according to most commentaries and scholars, this was not a parable. They know this for two reasons: first, no parable ever had a specific name in it, and this has two names: Abraham and Lazarus. In addition, Jesus said, "A *certain* rich man" (v. 1, emphasis added). And second, the most important and obvious reason that it is not a parable is because Jesus stated that "Abraham said" (v. 25). If Abraham didn't really say it, then Jesus was lying, because Abraham is the one giving the answer to the rich man. Jesus said that Abraham spoke, and Jesus doesn't lie. So it is clear this was not a parable.

However, even if it was a parable (and it wasn't), then tell me what does it mean? Jesus said that the man was in torment in the flame, and even the man himself said that he was in torment (vv. 23–24). Obviously there is pain in hell. The man also said that if a person would repent, they would avoid going to hell. He was concerned for his brothers; he didn't want them to end up there. So what would the lesson be from the parable if there really isn't a hell? If people do not go to hell and suffer there, then Jesus certainly conveyed the opposite meaning with His explanation. No, it is obviously a true story—and people will be, and are currently, in hell (Sheol or Hades). Revelation 20:13 states that "death and hell delivered up the dead which were in them: and they were judged every man according to their works." The word for "hell" used there is the word *Hades*. *Hades* is the Greek word for the present hell, the place where the rich man is. He will be delivered up at the Judgment Day and then thrown into the lake of fire (Rev. 20:15). So obviously the so-called parable's meaning is that people are in Hades suffering, and they do still exist.

The *Believer's Bible Commentary* tells us: "It should be noted that this is *not* spoken of as a parable."[1]

The *MacArthur Bible Commentary* states: "The beggar was the only character in any of Jesus' parables ever given a name. Some, therefore, have speculated that this was no imaginary tale, but an actual incident that really took place."[2]

Walter Martin writes: "...Christ, in parables, never used personal names, such as 'Lazarus.'...We must conclude, then, that Luke's account is a record of an actual case, a historical fact in which a soul suffered after death and was conscious of that torment.…There is a conscious punishment after death."[3]

*The New Testament Survey* tells us: "Some regard this account to be a parable, but if it is, it is the only parable in which a character is actually named. There is no reason to doubt that Jesus was speaking about a genuine historical experience."[4]

Christopher W. Morgan states: "In Luke 16:19–31, Jesus depicts hell as a place where justice prevails, consisting of suffering, torment, and agony (16:23–25, 27), and as a place of fire (16:24). Jesus graphically illustrates that this future punishment is final and inescapable separation and exclusion from heaven (16:25–26)."[5]

J. I. Packer states: "The fire of hell in the Bible is a picture not of destruction but of ongoing pain, as Luke 16:24 makes unambiguously clear."[6]

Finally, Robert A. Peterson states: "Lazarus, the penitent poor man, died, and went to 'Abraham's side,' where he was 'comforted' (Luke 16:22, 25).…By contrast, the impenitent rich man died and went to 'hell, where he was in torment…in agony in…fire.'…At death, Lazarus and the unsaved rich man left their bodies and went to places of bliss and woe, respectively."[7]

Here are some additional verses from Scripture about hell.

> » Deuteronomy 32:22: "For a fire is kindled in mine anger, and shall burn unto the lowest hell."

> » Job 15:30: "He shall *not depart out of darkness*; the flame shall dry up his branches" (emphasis added; this statement presupposes their existence).

» Job 18:15, 21: "Brimstone shall be scattered upon his habitation.... Surely such are the dwellings of the wicked." (One would need to exist in order to "dwell" in a place.)

» Psalm 9:17: "The wicked shall be turned into hell, and all the nations that forget God."

» Psalm 21:9: "Thou shalt make them as a fiery oven in the time of thine anger...the fire shall devour them."

» Psalm 49:19: "They shall never see light." (They must still exist in order to *never see* light.)

» Isaiah 14:9–10: "Hell from beneath is moved for thee to meet thee at thy coming.... They shall speak and say unto thee, Art thou also become weak as we?" (They must still exist to be able to speak.)

» Isaiah 33:12–14: "The people shall be as the burnings of lime: as thorns cut up shall they be burned in the fire.... Who among us shall dwell with the devouring fire? who among us shall dwell with everlasting burnings?" (How could one burn forever if they didn't exist?)

» Isaiah 34:10: "Not be quenched night nor day; the smoke thereof shall go up for ever."

» Isaiah 66:24: "For their worm shall not die, neither shall their fire be quenched; and they shall be an abhorring unto all flesh." (They must still exist to see them.)

» Ezekiel 31:14: "For they are all delivered unto death, to the nether parts of the earth, in the midst of the children of men, with them that go down to the pit."

» Ezekiel 31:16: "When I cast him down to hell with them that descend into the pit..."

» Ezekiel 32:21: "The strong among the mighty shall *speak* to him *out of the midst of hell*" (emphasis added; again, they are speaking in hell—they must still exist in order to speak).

» Daniel 12:2: "Some to everlasting life, and some to shame and everlasting contempt." (One would have to exist in order to experience everlasting shame and contempt.)

» Matthew 13:41–42: "They shall gather out of his kingdom all things that offend, and them which do iniquity; and shall cast them into a furnace of fire: there shall be wailing and gnashing of teeth." (They must exist in order to gnash their teeth.)

» Matthew 18:8: "...to be cast into everlasting fire." (Why have everlasting fire for nonexistent beings?)

» Mark 9:43: "...to go into hell, into the fire that never shall be quenched."

» Luke 13:24–28: "Strive to enter in at the strait gate: for many, I say unto you, will seek to enter in, and shall not be able....But he shall say, I tell you, I know you not whence ye are; depart from me, all ye workers of iniquity. There shall be weeping and gnashing of teeth, when ye shall see Abraham, and Isaac, and Jacob, and

*What Does the Bible Say About Hell?*

all the prophets, in the kingdom of God, and
you yourselves thrust out."

» Luke 16:23: "And in hell he lift up his eyes,
being in torments..."

» John 15:6: "Cast them into the fire, and they are
burned."

» 2 Thessalonians 1:7–9: "When the Lord Jesus
shall be revealed from heaven with his mighty
angels, in flaming fire taking vengeance on
them that know not God, and that obey not
the gospel of our Lord Jesus Christ: Who shall
be punished with everlasting destruction from
the presence of the Lord, and from the glory of
his power."

» Jude 7: "...suffering the vengeance of eternal
fire."

» Revelation 14:10–11: "He shall be tormented
with fire and brimstone in the presence of the
holy angels, and in the presence of the Lamb:
and the smoke of their torment ascendeth up
for ever and ever: and they have no rest day
nor night." (Some believe in annihilationism.
However, if people cease to exist after death,
then how do you explain that people are "in
His presence"—they must exist to be there!
Also, you have to exist to have "no rest day nor
night.")

» Revelation 20:13–14: "Death and hell delivered
up the dead which were in them: and they were
judged every man according to their works."
(How can hell deliver up those which were in

them if they do not exist? And how can they be judged—and why would they be judged—if they were simply annihilated? There are also many verses on degrees of punishment—see Matthew 10:15; 16:27; 23:14–15; Luke 12:47; and Hebrews 10:28–29. Why would there be varying degrees of punishment if all are annihilated as some people teach?)

» Revelation 21:8: "But the fearful, and unbelieving, and the abominable, and murderers, and whoremongers, and sorcerers, and idolaters, and all liars, shall have their part in the lake which burneth with fire and brimstone."

(Also see Proverbs 9:18; Isaiah 30:33; 38:17–18; 45:16; Jeremiah 20:11; Malachi 4:1; Luke 3:17; 2 Peter 2:17; Jude 13.)

There are many more verses in the Bible about hell and destruction. I have an appendix in my book *Hell*, listing approximately 250 verses on the subject. Why would anyone want to risk their eternal soul on simply an opinion and ignore so many verses written in a trusted and proven book from God Almighty?

Some have asked why hell is so horrible. Why did God make such a terrible place? I explained this in my book *23 Questions About Hell* and also in the book *Hell*. However, I will give a brief answer here to this question. First, hell was prepared for the devil and his angels, not for man (Matt. 25:41). Second, because all good comes from God (James 1:17), it then follows that to be apart from Him there remains no good thing. Hell is a place that is separated from His goodness or His attributes (Prov. 15:29; 2 Thess. 1:9–10).

Randy Alcorn states: "Because God is the source of all good, and Hell is the absence of God, Hell must also be the absence of all good."[8] Robert A. Peterson writes, "God is everywhere present, he is present in hell. Although he is not there in grace and blessing, he is there in holiness and wrath."[9]

There are only two places created to last for eternity, and if man rejects the only way into heaven, then there remains no other place to go but hell. God cannot annihilate anyone because we are made in His image, created to last forever (Gen. 1:26). God will not break His Word, nor will He change what He has already spoken (Ps. 89:34; 119:89). In Matthew 25:46 Jesus said, "And these shall go away into everlasting punishment: but the righteous into life eternal." The word for "eternal" is *aionios*. Jesus used the same word for both places in the original Greek. Since those in heaven are eternal, so are those in hell. Jesus used the phrase "everlasting punishment." The word for "punishment" is the word *kolasis*, which means "torment." How can one be tormented if they do not exist, as some teach?

Many today no longer believe in a place of torment, at least not for "good" people. The reason is they cannot reconcile a loving God with One who would allow everlasting punishment. Therefore, they resort to embracing nonbiblical teachings, such as annihilationism or universalism. Some have not heard a clear explanation on why hell is justifiable. But there are clear answers to these questions, and I have answered many of them in my book *23 Questions About Hell* and in *Hell: Separate the Truth From Fiction*, and also in this book that you are holding! The books *Hell Under Fire*, written by nine very accredited and well-respected scholars, and *Hell on Trial*, also written by one of those scholars, answer questions and refute many of these false teachings in a thorough and authoritative manner. After reading the answers and reasons given in these resources, hopefully you will realize that your questioning of God's justice was simply out of a lack of knowledge. The Bible states all throughout that God is just. Deuteronomy 32:4 states, "For all his ways are judgment: a God of truth and without iniquity, just and right is he." Acts 17:31 states: "He will judge the world in righteousness." And Psalm 33:4–5 tells us: "For the Word of the LORD is right; and all his works are done in truth. He loveth righteousness and judgment."

Wayne Grudem again states: "Scripture clearly affirms that God will be entirely just in his judgment and no one will be able to complain against him on that day."[10] Walter Martin explains: "…because He is Love, He is also *Justice* and must require infinite retribution upon anyone who treads underfoot the precious blood of Christ, who is the Lamb slain for lost sinners from the foundation of the world."[11] Finally, Christopher W. Morgan writes: "God's love does not drive his justice. The implementation of God's justice does not undermine his love. God's love and justice cohere." He then quotes Jonathan Edwards as saying, "It is an unreasonable and unscriptural notion of the mercy of God that He is merciful in such a sense that He cannot bear that penal justice should be excused."[12]

Some have asked if punishment for the lost is all the same in hell. No, the Scripture is clear that there are different levels of torment and degrees of punishment. Jesus said the following:

> » Matthew 10:15: "It shall be more tolerable for the land of Sodom and Gomorrah in the day of judgment, than for that city." (Jesus was inferring there is a less tolerable judgment.)

> » Matthew 16:27: "For the Son of man shall come in the glory of his Father with his angels; and then he shall reward every man according to his works."

» Matthew 23:14: "Ye shall receive the greater damnation." (This infers a lesser damnation!)

» Matthew 23:15: "Ye make him twofold more the child of hell than yourselves."

» Luke 12:47–48: "...beaten with many stripes... beaten with few stripes."

» Hebrews 10:29: "Of how much sorer punishment, suppose ye, shall he be thought worthy, who hath trodden under foot the Son of God." (A worse punishment infers a lesser one exists.)

» Revelation 20:13: "...and they were judged every man according to their works."

If annihilation or universalism were true, then how could you explain these statements of Jesus? How could there be degrees of punishment if all are annihilated, or if no one was even in hell? The truth is that any level in hell is horrendous because it is separation from God—and all of life.

Dr. Chuck Missler says:

> The wicked are resurrected and consigned to their eternal state....Men will be held accountable because of Creation. That alone is enough to consign them to their eternal punishment....People who deny God are doing it as a decision. It's not an intellectual thing, it's a choice thing....We know the punishment is conscious....We have no ability to imagine what it's like without hope.[13]

Dr. Missler goes on:

> A God deserving of worship cannot issue an arbitrary amnesty for humanitarians or pantheists who

persist in worshiping and serving themselves more than their personal Creator Himself. The condemnation of everyone who was lost will be wholly contributable to himself, or herself, having disregarded God's revealed will, and his will is sufficiently revealed in Creation itself.[14]

Some think that God is "mean" for allowing people to suffer in hell. But remember, the God you are accusing of being mean is the same God who suffered a horrible death on the cross to keep us out of hell! What more do you want Him to do? Besides, as I already pointed out, God doesn't send anyone to hell. Jesus said that it's our own words that condemn us (Matt. 12:37).

Edward Donnelly writes:

> Hell brings us to our knees, moving us to wonder and gratitude. Hell inspires us with a new adoration for him who loved us and gave himself for us. His death destroyed and cancelled hell for us. That is what he is worth; that is who he is.[15]

Why would any rationally thinking person risk their soul by betting on the possibility that Jesus was lying? God is a just and fair God, and He gives everyone countless opportunities to accept His Son throughout their lives. No one will be in hell because they didn't know. They knew the way to heaven, but they decided to reject the truth (Rom. 1:21–32). They push Him away, over and over again. They *choose* to reject Jesus Christ as their Lord and Savior by refusing to repent of their sins.

Here are some quotes from some scholars and early church fathers:

We set aside the error of those who say that the punishment of the wicked are to be ended at some time.... Therefore an infinite punishment is deserved for a sin committed against Him.[16]

—THOMAS AQUINAS

Hence, because the eternal life of the saints will be endless, the eternal punishment also, for those condemned to it, will assuredly have no end.[17]

—AUGUSTINE

Impenitent sinners in hell shall have end without end, death without death, night without day, mourning without mirth, sorrow without solace, and bondage without liberty. The damned shall live as long in hell as God Himself shall live in Heaven.[18]

—THOMAS BROOKS

Everlasting destruction and the torment of the flesh await all those whom he will drive from his presence at the last day.... We ought to represent to our minds the future vengeance of God against the wicked, which, being more grievous than all earthly torments, ought rather to excite horror than a desire to know it. But we must observe the eternity of this fire...[19]

—JOHN CALVIN

Concerning the endless punishment of those who will die impenitent...Eternal punishment is not eternal annihilation. Surely they will not be raised to life at the last day only to be annihilated.[20]

—JONATHAN EDWARDS

Since when believers die they pass immediately into the presence of God, and when unbelievers die they pass into a state of separation from God and the endurance of punishment…[21]

—WAYNE GRUDEM

There is a Hebrew word that can only be translated "grave" (*kever*), but the writers often preferred the word *sheol* because it encompassed the region of departed spirits who were conscious, either in bliss or torment.[22]

—ERWIN W. LUTZER

There is a place and state of everlasting misery in the other world where there is nothing but weeping and gnashing of teeth, which speaks the souls tribulation and anguish under God's indignation and wrath.[23]

—MATTHEW HENRY

A decisive proof is that there is a hell for the body as well as the soul in the eternal world; in other words, that the torment that awaits the lost will have elements of suffering adapted to the material as well as the spiritual part of our nature, both of which, we are assured, will exist forever.[24]

—*COMMENTARY ON THE WHOLE BIBLE*

The scriptures, however, clearly state that those who reject Christ's mercies during this life will endure an eternity in hell while fully conscious forever.[25]

—GRANT JEFFREY

The fiery oven is ignited merely by the unbearable appearance of God and endures eternally…. Constantly, the damned will be judged, constantly they will suffer pain, and constantly they will be a fiery oven, that is, they will be tortured.[26]

—MARTIN LUTHER

We find Scripture is clear in its teaching that those who reject God's salvation will suffer throughout eternity in outer darkness.... The Bible teaches that unregenerate mankind will suffer the eternal wrath of God and must undergo destruction and ruin of their original function...[27]

—WALTER MARTIN

The agents of suffering never end because those in hell experience conscious suffering forever.... This brief overview clearly demonstrates that the future punishment of the wicked in hell is a significant theme in the New Testament.... In fact, future punishment is addressed in some way by every New Testament author.... The chief description of hell in the New Testament is punishment.... The punishment also consists of suffering. Those in hell suffer intense and excruciating pain.[28]

—CHRISTOPHER W. MORGAN

So eternal punishment means a divine penal infliction that is ultimate in the same sense in which eternal life is ultimate—prima facie, therefore, everlasting and unending.... Matthew 25:46, said O. C. Quick, Regius Professor of Theology at Oxford, is one of the two most explicit New Testament texts affirming permanent penal pain for some after death.[29]

—J. I. PACKER

Startling as it may sound, it is nevertheless a fact, that the Scriptures speak much more frequently of

God's anger and wrath, than they do of His love and compassion. To argue, then, that because God is love, He will not inflict eternal torment on the wicked, is to ignore the fact that God is light, and is to asperse His holiness....Moreover, to deny the justice of eternal punishment is to fly in the face of Christian consciousness.[30]

—A. W. PINK

...We speak of the wrath to come, and everlasting punishment which God apportions to the unrepentant, with fear and trembling, but we speak of it because we cannot escape from correction that it is taught in the Word of God.[31]

—C. H. SPURGEON

...the fire of hell is eternal—expressly announced as an everlasting penalty, and let him then admit that it is from this circumstance that this never-ending "killing" is more formidable than a merely human murder, which is only temporal.[32]

—TERTULLIAN

Hell is a place and it's eternal. One hundred thirty-two texts prove such a place is real.[33]

—JACK VAN IMPE

That very moment that the soul is separated from the body; in that instant the soul loses all those pleasures whose enjoyment depends on the outward senses. The smell, the taste, the touch delight no more....In the dreary regions of the dead all these things are forgotten....There is no grandeur in the infernal regions; there is nothing beautiful in those dark abodes; no light except that of livid flames. And nothing new: just one unvaried scene of horror upon horror! There is no music but that of groans and shrieks; of weeping, wailing, and gnashing of teeths...No; they are the heirs of shame and everlasting contempt. Thus they are totally separated from all the things they were found of in the present world...for there is no friendship in hell....But it has been questioned by some whether there is any fire in hell: that is, any material fire. Indeed, if there is any fire, it is unquestionably material....Does not our Lord speak as if it were real fire? No one can deny or doubt of this: Is it possible then to suppose that the God of truth would speak in this manner if it were not so? Does He design to fright His poor creatures? What! With scarecrows? With vain shadows of things that have no being? O let not anyone think so! Do not impute such folly to the Most High.[34]

—John Wesley

People who die today, without Christ, go to Hades. It is a place of torment where demons (evil spirits) torment people in various chambers and the intensity of the punishment received depends on the sins they committed.[35]

—Theo Wolmarans

Hell is a literal place, just as heaven is. It is not metaphorical or allegorical, as some say. The Bible is clear, and we should take it literally as God meant it to be taken.

# 14

# Have You Invested in Heaven?

OST OF US invest in our future. We plan, save, and strategize to be debt free and to have something for our retirement years. Yet not many people even consider investing in their eternity. The retirement years are few, but eternity is a long time. It would be prudent to have an eternal perspective and invest into our life beyond this temporal existence. As David Shibley states: "But if we view this life as a sort of boot camp for the afterlife, our perceptions—and our actions—will change. Our true allegiance will be to the kingdom of heaven."[1]

Jesus said in Matthew 6:19–21, "Lay not up for yourselves treasures upon earth, where moth and rust doth corrupt, and where thieves break through and steal: but lay up for yourselves treasures in heaven, where neither moth nor rust doth corrupt, and where thieves do not break through nor steal: For where your treasure is, there will your heart be also."

The question is, what are treasures in heaven? One of the treasures would be what Jesus said in Matthew 19:21: "If thou wilt be perfect, go and sell that thou hast, and give to the poor, and thou shalt have treasure in heaven: and come and follow me." In giving to the poor you will store up for yourself treasure not only in heaven, but also on the earth. Proverbs 28:27 states: "He that giveth unto the poor shall not lack…" Also Psalm 41:1–2 tells us: "Blessed is he that considereth the poor: the LORD will deliver him in time of trouble. The LORD will preserve him, and keep him alive; and he shall be blessed upon the earth." To give to the poor will also bring us eternal rewards.

In chapter 8 I mentioned some of the rewards we will receive in heaven, such as ruling over cities, or over nations, or over other events as the Scriptures declare. The great rewards will be given to those who were servants of the Lord (Matt. 5:12, 19; 6:18; 11:11; 18:4; 20:27; 23:11; 25:23; Luke 19:16–17; 22:27; Rev. 2:26).

The most important investment we can make into heaven is to bring people with us. We can take nothing with us when we die—except for other souls. Again, Jesus stated that if a man has one hundred sheep, and one goes astray, he will go after the one and rejoice much when the one is found (Matt. 18:12). Jesus went on to explain in Matthew 18:14: "Even so it is not the will of your Father which is in heaven, that one of these little ones should perish." He was showing the importance of one soul that is saved, how precious that one soul is to God. Psalm 49:8 tells us: "For the redemption of their soul is precious." Jesus said, "There is joy in the presence of the angels of God over one sinner that repenteth" (Luke 15:10). First Corinthians 9:22 states: "I am made all things to all men, that I might by all means save some." And Proverbs 11:30 states: "He that winneth souls is wise."

It takes effort to share the gospel with others, and many times there is opposition to our witness. It is easier for us as Christians to read our Bibles, go to church, and then do little else. But God wants us to have His perspective and try to influence as many people as possible in order for them to come into the kingdom. One of the ways to be a good witness for Jesus is to be aware of how we perform our jobs. Jentezen Franklin writes: "Don't be a slacker, because that's your witness. Jesus said, 'Let your light so shine before men, that they may see your good works, and glorify your Father which is in heaven' (Matt. 5:16). What? They see how you work, and that gives you a platform into their life. If you want to witness to your boss, give an extra effort every day, and the opportunity will come for you. Then he'll respect your witness."[2]

God desires to bless people, and it is up to us to open our mouths and share the way of salvation.

Jesus told us in Mark 16:15: "Go ye into all the world, and preach the gospel to every creature." This is not a suggestion, but a command.

Charles W. Spurgeon said: "Soul winning is the chief business of the Christian; indeed, it should be the main pursuit of every true believer."[3]

It is interesting that, as people get close to death, it is usually easier to talk to them about the afterlife. Dr. Maurice Rawlings states: "To my knowledge, I have never seen a dying atheist."[4]

It is an unfortunate fact that many times it takes a tragedy, severe illness, or some other catastrophic event to be able to have a conversation with someone about God and the afterlife. I suppose many people think that any discussion about God will cramp their lifestyles, so the conversation is put off until they are faced with something serious.

Usually people will make some preparations for death. We prepare a will or we set up a trust fund. We carefully consider our final plans, visit with our families, and say all the important things we need to say to our loved ones. Some people desire to see a priest or person of the cloth when they are on their deathbeds. They are usually in fear when they are at the point of death, as I have observed so many times in visiting them in the hospital. If a person does not know Jesus, there is usually an overwhelming fear that comes over them. And they should be glad it does, as this fear places them in a position to listen and be open to the truth (Job 33:15–22). Jude 23 tells us: "And others save with fear, pulling them out of the fire." That is the only time some are willing to talk about and listen to the way to heaven. If we are already a Christian, then we know we are ready to leave this life. We have peace with God in our hearts because we are trusting in Him. As a Christian, we have full assurance of our salvation and our eternal destiny (Isa. 51:6; Acts 17:31; Heb. 5:9; 1 John 2:25).

The one thing a Christian normally desires more than anything else before they pass on is to be certain that their families are also Christians. The rich man came to realize when he arrived in hell that his brothers needed to repent of their sins, or they too would end up in that horrible place of torment (Luke 16:30). He was concerned for them and didn't want them to suffer as he was suffering. Billy Graham reports what one man stated in his will: "...here is what Patrick Henry wrote in his will: 'I have now disposed of all my property to my family. There is one thing more I wish I could give them, and that is faith in Jesus Christ. If they had that and I had not given them one shilling, they would be rich; and if I had not given them that, and had given them all the world, they would be poor indeed.'"[5]

Jesus said, "For what is a man profited, if he shall gain the whole world, and lose his own soul? or what shall a man give in exchange for his soul?" (Matt. 16:26).

We cannot force God's love and forgiveness upon anyone. We can only share God's plan of salvation, and each person must decide for themselves. We need to pray that people will discover the truth before it's too late—like it was for the rich man in hell.

The following illustration gives us an eternal perspective, as written by R. Wayne Wills: "Louis Pasteur, the pioneer of immunology, lived at a time when thousands of people died each year of rabies. Pasteur had worked for years on a vaccine. Just as he was about to begin experimenting on himself, a nine-year-old, Joseph Meister, was bitten by a rabid dog. The boy's mother begged Pasteur to experiment on her son. Pasteur injected Joseph for ten days—and the boy lived. Decades later, [out of] all of the things Pasteur could have had etched on his headstone, he asked for three words: JOSEPH MEISTER LIVED. Our greatest legacy will be those who live eternally because of our efforts."[6]

When we arrive in heaven and see those whom we helped influence to see the light and accept the Lord, it will be a most valued reward.

The Bible states that there are also many rewards given in heaven to those who were obedient on the earth.

- » Psalm 19:11: "…and in keeping of them [commandments] there is great reward."

- » Psalm 62:12: "…for thou renderest to every man according to his work."

- » Proverbs 11:18: "…but to him that soweth righteousness shall be a sure reward."

- » Proverbs 13:13: "…but he that feareth the commandment shall be rewarded."

- » Jeremiah 31:16: "…for thy work shall be rewarded."

- » Hosea 4:9: "…and I will punish them for their ways, and reward them their doings."

- » Matthew 5:11–12: "Blessed are ye, when men shall revile you, and persecute you…for my sake. Rejoice, and be exceeding glad: for great is your reward in heaven…"

» Matthew 6:1, 4: "Take heed that ye do not your alms before men, to be seen of them: otherwise ye have no reward of your Father which is in heaven...and thy Father which seeth in secret himself shall reward thee openly."

» Matthew 16:27: "...and then he shall reward every man according to his works."

» Mark 9:41: "For whosoever shall give you a cup of water to drink in my name, because ye belong to Christ, verily I say unto you, he shall not lose his reward."

» Luke 6:23: "...your reward is great in heaven" (i.e., when men hate you for Jesus's sake).

» Luke 14:13-14: "But when thou makest a feast, call the poor, the maimed, the lame, the blind: and thou shalt be blessed; for they cannot recompense thee: for thou shalt be recompensed at the resurrection of the just."

» 1 Corinthians 3:8: "...and every man shall receive his own reward according to his own labour."

» 1 Corinthians 3:14: "...he shall receive a reward."

» Colossians 3:24: "Knowing that of the Lord ye shall receive the reward of the inheritance: for ye serve the Lord Christ."

» Hebrews 11:6: "...he is a rewarder of them that diligently seek him."

» Revelation 11:18: "...thou shouldest give reward unto thy servants the prophets, and to the saints, and them that fear thy name..."

> » Revelation 22:12: "And my reward is with me, to give every man according as his work shall be."

> » Other verses that speak to our eternal rewards include Psalm 58:11; Matthew 6:6; Luke 6:35; Hebrews 10:32–35; 2 John 8.

As Christians, do we have an eternal perspective? Are we concerned about those who do not know the way of salvation? Are we doing things that will count for eternity?

Billy Graham writes: "Five minutes after [I'm in heaven]… Suddenly the things I thought important—tomorrow's tasks, the plans for the dinner at my church, my success or failure in pleasing those around me—these will matter not at all. And the things to which I gave but little thought—the word about Christ to the man next door, the moment (how short it was) of earnest prayer for the Lord's work in far-off lands, the confessing and forsaking of that secret sin—will stand as real and enduring. Five minutes after I'm in heaven, I'll be overwhelmed by the truths I've known but somehow never grasped. I'll realize then that it's what I am in Christ that comes first with God…"[7]

Will we choose to live for God, or will we choose to live for ourselves? We are not giving up anything of value to live for God, and He even rewards us if we do. It is not a loss, but much gain. It is scriptural for us to desire the rewards He promises.

David Shibley writes: "Every now and then I run across people who will say, 'Well, I'm not doing this for rewards. It will be reward enough just to be in heaven.' This misses the whole point—and it's bad theology. Heaven is not a reward; it is part of our redemption gift package when we come to saving faith in Jesus Christ. Further, to place little value on what heaven says has great value insults the very Lord who offers these rewards."[8]

Jesus actually told us in the Sermon on the Mount that we will obtain rewards (Luke 6:23). If you have a problem with this, you may need to change and acquire the mind of Christ (Eph. 4:23; Phil. 2:5).

Charles H. Spurgeon wrote: "At the mention of the word *reward*, some will prick up their ears and mutter, 'Legality.' Yet the reward we speak of is not of debt, but of grace. It is not enjoyed with the proud conceit of merit, but with the grateful delight of humility."[9]

In his book one of the things Spurgeon is talking about is rewards given to those who witness for Christ. He goes on to say: "However, the richest reward lies in pleasing God and causing the Redeemer to see the results of the travail of His soul. That Jesus should have His reward is worthy of the eternal Father, but it is marvelous that we would be employed by the Father to give to Christ the purchase of His agonies. This is a wonder of wonders!"[10] In other words, the fact that we could contribute to Jesus's reward by winning souls is truly astonishing.

Moses also appreciated the reward given, "for he had respect unto the recompence of the reward" (Heb. 11:26).

Another of the greatest rewards we could be given in heaven will be time allowed with Jesus. To be able to walk and talk with Him would be the most precious gift of all. Could it be, perhaps, that the more time we spend with Him in prayer here, the more time we will have with Him in heaven? It is not that we could ever earn it, but the Bible does say, "...he is a rewarder of them that diligently seek him" (Heb. 11:6). In addition, Galatians 6:7 says, "...for whatsoever a man soweth, that shall he also reap." If we sow time with Him here, will we reap more time with Him in heaven? Just a thought!

# 15

# Losing Life to Find It!

J ESUS SAID IN Matthew 10:39, "He that findeth his life shall lose it: and he that loseth his life for my sake shall find it." What did Jesus mean by that statement? The natural tendency is for us to live selfish lives, and to place ourselves first. Jesus was talking about surrendering our own ways and submitting to His will. Jesus also said in Matthew 16:24, "If any man will come after me, let him deny himself, and take up his cross, and follow me." He also said to "take up his cross daily…" (Luke 9:23). He said in Matthew 10:38: "And he that taketh not his cross, and followeth after me, is not worthy of me." He continued, "And whosoever doth not bear his cross, and come after me, cannot be my disciple" (Luke 14:27). In Luke 14:26–28 Jesus explained that we must count the cost first, and if we don't "hate" our loved ones and our own lives in comparison to Him, we cannot be His disciple (Mark 8:34–35; 10:21). That does not sound like a person asking for a partial commitment. Jesus is forthright, strong, and direct about how we are to serve Him. No compromise here!

The *Believer's Bible Commentary* states it this way:

> The temptation is to hug one's life by trying to avoid the pain and loss of a life of total commitment. But this is the greatest waste of a life—to spend it in the gratification of self. The greatest use of a life is to spend it in the service of Christ. The person who

166

loses his life in devotedness to Him will find it in its true fullness.[1]

Rod Parsley states:

> So while America's liberal churches have abandoned the preaching of the cross because of its focus on sin and repentance, many of her conservative evangelical churches have shied away from it because of its unpopular call for self-denial and sacrifice.... When we begin with the message, "God loves you and has a wonderful plan for your life," should we be surprised that many enter the kingdom thinking, *Of course, it's all about me.*[2]

In Proverbs 18:2 Solomon states: "A fool hath no delight in understanding, but that his heart may discover itself." In other words, a fool is only concerned with his own self and his own personal opinion. There is selfishness in America in general, and it now even permeates our churches.

Rod Parsley goes on to say:

> Is it any wonder most evangelical churches today can't even get people to work in the nursery once a month—much less reach out to drug addicts or struggling single mothers? They have never been told that to save your life, you must lose it.[3]

John Bevere gives us this challenge:

> Jesus makes it clear that to follow Him, we must first count the cost. There is a price to following Jesus, and He makes the amount certain. The price is nothing short of our lives![4]

Glen Berteau writes:

> Today many Christians are convinced that Jesus
> Christ came to earth to make them happy and suc-
> cessful....But Jesus didn't come to make us feel
> better about our selfishness and sins. He came
> to forgive our sins, transform us, and change our
> hearts so we find sin detestable instead of desirable.[5]

How do we lose our life in Him and change our desires?
As we read His Word daily, our minds are renewed day
by day, and we fall more and more in love with Him. (See
2 Corinthians 4:16; Ephesians 4:23; James 1:21.) John Bevere
continues: "You can only love someone to the extent that you
know them."[6] We can only get to know God by spending
time with Him in prayer and in His Word.

Now, many think that if they commit their lives to serving
God, then they have to give up all they enjoy and move to
some remote jungle somewhere to be a missionary. He is not
asking us to give up all we love, but rather, to surrender ourselves to His perfect will. He wants us to use our entire God-
given abilities for His purpose. And as far as moving to the
jungle, God has made each one of us different. He knows
whether we are capable of handling it. And, if not, then He
usually wouldn't ask us to go. I will elaborate on that point
just ahead. But first, God has given us individual desires, talents, and destinies. When each one of us submits to God's
will for our lives, we start noticing a certain desire or an
inclination toward something. You might desire to help in
the child-care department in your church or even do the
camera work for the church. You might want to be on the
street witnessing team. Your call from God might not even
be in the ministry world at all. It might be as an accountant,
in helping people to save and handle money. It might be as

a lawyer, to defend the innocent. It could be in politics, to help combat some of the attacks against Christianity or to help govern fairly. If your call actually is in the ministry, it could be overseas or in your own backyard. My wife and I met one couple who is in the ministry in the roughest parts of Africa. They live in the jungle, have to keep their heads shaved because of the lice, and eat many strange foods, but they love it. They told me they could never do what we do, wearing a suit and traveling in airplanes, sleeping indoors, and so forth. God gives each man the desire to do what He has equipped them for. He won't place you in something you are not built for. So there is no need to be fearful of submitting yourself to God's will for your life, as His will is the best thing for you.

Now, on the other hand, that doesn't mean it will always be exactly what you want. Many times He pulls us out of our comfort zone, and we may be doing something we would not desire in the least! However, after a while, we will become comfortable with God's will. We will discover that He has equipped us for the job.

As for my wife and me, we never wanted to travel, as we like our routine. Traveling completely disrupts a systematic lifestyle. In addition, the last thing I ever wanted to do was to be a public speaker. On top of that, I am a conservative person who would never want to be identified with those who say they have had some kind of supernatural experience. I have been conservative all my life, and I gravitate to the more scholarly teachers of the Bible. I have had my own real estate business for thirty-five years, which is a conservative profession. Also, I have been a person who enjoys the background; I do not like to be in front of large crowds, on TV, and so forth. So you see, I had to be willing to trust God with my life, and then later on, I became comfortable with these things. However, it did take awhile, I might add. But now, I wouldn't want to do anything else. Of course, God knew that, and I didn't even realize that I would be capable of such things. Now, back to what it means to place God first in our lives.

Jesus said in Matthew 19:29: "And every one that hath forsaken houses, or brethren, or sisters, or father, or mother, or wife, or children, or lands, for my name's sake, shall receive an hundredfold, and shall inherit everlasting life." He is saying that if you give up anything for Him, you will receive a hundred times what you gave up, and you will also have the joy of entering heaven. God will never be out-given, since He is always the giver of every good thing we have (James 1:17). Jesus also said in Mark 9:35, "If any man desire to be first, the same shall be last of all, and servant of all."

We should strive to always be in God's perfect will, whatever that entails. Each one of us is called to share the good news of the gospel. The world is won over to Christ one person at a time, and we all can participate. The Bible says that "he that winneth souls is wise" (Prov. 11:30). And Jesus said in Mark 16:15, "Go ye into all the world, and preach the gospel to every creature." If we can influence a person toward heaven, it is a treasure in God's sight, and it will bring us a great reward.

# 16

# Is It Really My Own Words?

J ESUS SAID IN Matthew 12:37, "For by thy words thou shalt be justified, and by thy words thou shalt be condemned." He told us that our own words send us to hell, and not Him. Why does He say that? Revelation 21:8 states that all unbelievers will be cast into the lake of fire. If we say with our own mouth, "I don't believe God or what He said in the Bible. I believe in my own opinion," then we would be in disagreement with what Jesus said *is* the only way to heaven. If we do not make a decision for Christ, then we send ourselves to hell. Also, a non-decision doesn't mean we are on the fence or in a neutral position. A non-decision is, in fact, a decision. It would be hell by default! We must confess Jesus as our Lord and Savior in order to be saved (Rom. 10:9–10). Otherwise our own words will condemn us to hell. Of course, it is God who carries out the actual ordering of the executioners to send the person to hell (Job 33:22—the word there is "sheol" and not "grave"). Just as in a court sentencing, the judge is the one who gives the orders, but it is only because the person is first found guilty.

As Christians, we will also be judged for our words: not in the sense of salvation, but in regard to our rewards (2 Cor. 5:10–11). R. T. Kendall points out: "Could I give you what is perhaps my most 'unfavorite' verse in the Bible? It is Matthew 12:36—the words of Jesus: 'I tell you that men will have to give account on the day of judgment for every

171

careless word they have spoken.'...Oh, dear! I am in serious trouble....I cannot think of anything scarier than having every careless word, idle word, useless word, or thoughtless word thrown up at me on that day....Were we to believe it literally, I can assure you that it would go a long way in helping us to control our tongues."[1] That is truly a very scary verse for all of us!

All of us, above the age of accountability (which varies for each of us; the Bible doesn't give a specific age, other than a hint in Isaiah 7:15–16, that it is when a person knows good from evil) are automatically on the road to hell. John 3:18 states that we are "condemned already, because he hath not believed in the name of the only begotten Son of God." In addition, because we are all born in sin, we are all eternally separated from God (Ps. 51:1–5; Rom. 3:10, 12, 23; 5:12–14). We have to be given a new heart and a new spirit (Ezek. 11:19; 18:31; 36:26; 2 Cor. 5:17). That only comes through trusting in Jesus Christ as our Lord and Savior. We have to say with our own mouth, as Romans 10:9 instructs: "That if thou shalt confess with thy mouth the Lord Jesus, and shalt believe in thine heart that God hath raised him from the dead, thou shalt be saved." Jesus said in Luke 13:5: "Except ye repent, ye shall all likewise perish." To turn away from our sin is a requirement for salvation. It is saying we are sorry for our sins (2 Cor. 7:9). We cannot do that on our own, but when we receive Him, He gives us the grace to be able to resist sin. We hopefully will mature in our walk with Him and eventually grow to hate sin (Ps. 97:10; 119:113, 128; Prov. 8:13; Rom. 6:6, 12, 14). Our trust in Him for our salvation is considered as righteousness (Rom. 5:18; 2 Cor. 5:21; Titus 3:5). Also, we do not need to clean ourselves up first. We just come as we are. Arthur Blessitt says, "No one is too sinful or too far gone. God will hear the prayer of anyone who wants to know Him, whether that person is a Muslim, a Jew, a Hindu, a Buddhist, an atheist, or a member of a Christian Church who doesn't have a relationship with Jesus."[2]

Revelation 20:15 says, "And whosoever was not found written in the book of life was cast into the lake of fire."

The question I have for you is this: Do you know if your name is written in God's book? You might want to know now, rather than find out later, when it will be too late.

## Prayer for Receiving Jesus Into Your Heart

If you want your name written in His book, you can know that it is there right now by saying this prayer. What you are doing is making a commitment to Him. It will mean a changed lifestyle—and a turning away from sin. If you are ready, then say this prayer out loud:

*Dear God in heaven,*

*I know that I have sinned, and I cannot save myself. I believe You sent Your Son, Jesus, to die on a cross for me. I believe He was crucified, died, and was buried, but He rose from the dead, and He lives forevermore. I know my works cannot save me, but only by the shed blood of Jesus on the cross can I have my sins washed away. I ask You to come into my heart, and I receive You as my Lord and Savior. You are the Son of the living God. Thank You, Jesus, for coming into my life. Thank You, God, for saving me! I now confess that I am a born-again Christian, going to heaven, in Jesus's name I pray, amen. (See Luke 13:3; John 3:3, 16; Acts 4:12; Romans 3:23, 25; 5:8, 12; 6:23; 10:9–10; 1 Corinthians 15:3–4; 1 John 1:7.)*

If you said that prayer today, praise God and then go and tell someone about it. Jesus said, "Whosoever therefore shall confess me before men, him will I confess also before my Father which is in heaven" (Matt. 10:32). Now this is only the beginning. Two things are important to do. The first is to read the Bible every day. This is not a religious exercise. The Bible is a manual for life. Through it you will learn about this wonderful Jesus we serve. The Bible teaches us how to live life successfully and how to overcome the difficult issues we all face. It teaches us how to obtain the promises of God, which come by obedience to His Word. Second, it is so important to go to a church that teaches the Bible. We need to learn to pray. We also need to fellowship with others who will be like-minded, and we need to pray with others. Listening to teaching CDs daily will strengthen us, and it is essential for a healthy Christian life. Thank you for your commitment to the Lord and for reading this book. May the Lord bless you and use you in a powerful way to help others.

# 17

# Baptism—Is It a Requirement?

THE BIBLE ALSO instructs us to be baptized in water. This should be done as soon as possible. It is an outward sign to show we have put our flesh under, and we put it to death, identifying with Christ's death. This is not a requirement for salvation, but we are instructed throughout the New Testament to do so. Now some will disagree and state that it is a requirement to be saved. I will address this issue now, rather than hear from those who will want to try and correct me. It is not a requirement, as the Scripture makes so clear. In addition, almost every reputable scholar, commentary, and denomination makes it clear that water baptism is not a requirement for salvation.

Let's look at some proofs of this fact in the Bible. Acts 10:45–48 says, "... on the Gentiles also was poured out the gift of the Holy Ghost. For they heard them speak with tongues, and magnify God. Then answered Peter, Can any man forbid water, that these should not be baptized, which have received the Holy Ghost as well as we? And he commanded them to be baptized in the name of the Lord." Now that is about as clear as you can get. They were not only saved, but also filled with the Holy Ghost and spoke in tongues before they were baptized.

In addition, as the *Believer's Bible Commentary* points out: "Jesus himself did not baptize (John 4:1–2)—a strange omission if baptism were necessary for salvation. Paul thanked God that he baptized very few of the Corinthians (1 Cor. 1:14–16)—an impossible thanksgiving if baptism were essential for salvation. Approximately 150 passages in the [New Testament] state that salvation is by faith alone. No verse or few verses could contradict this overwhelming testimony. Baptism is connected with death and burial in the [New Testament], not with spiritual birth."[1]

There are thirty-four verses that mention repentance. But only three out of the thirty-four mention repentance with baptism! One of these instances I will explain just ahead. The remaining thirty verses speak of repentance only.

Here are the thirty references of the verses that mention repentance only, with no mention of baptism: Matthew 3:2, 8; 4:17; 9:13; Mark 1:4, 15; 2:17; 6:12; Luke 3:3, 8; 5:32; 13:3, 5; 15:7; 16:30; 17:3–4; 24:47; Acts 3:19; 8:22; 13:24; 17:30; 20:21; 26:20; Revelation 2:5, 16, 21–22; 3:3, 19.

The *Believer's Bible Commentary* mentions that there are one hundred fifty verses that state salvation is by faith alone. Here are just thirteen of those verses: Romans 3:22, 25, 28, 30; 4:5, 16; 5:1; 11:20; Galatians 2:16; 3:8; 2 Timothy 3:15; Hebrews 6:12; and 1 Peter 1:5.

The overwhelming number of these verses must take priority over the mere three that mention baptism and repentance together. And even those three have an explanation, which I will address in relation to one of them.

The strongest verse used by those who support baptism as a requirement for salvation is Mark 16:16, which reads: "He that believeth and is baptized shall be saved; but he that believeth not shall be damned."

*Nelson's New Illustrated Bible Commentary* has this to say about this verse: "He who does not believe will be condemned. This negative statement shows that baptism is not a requirement for salvation. Otherwise the statement would read that he who does not believe and is not baptized will be condemned."[2]

*Believer's Bible Commentary* says this: "Baptism is not a condition of salvation, but an outward proclamation that the person has been saved."[3]

*The Encyclopedia of Bible Words* tells us: "Certainly the early church did not see water baptism as necessary for salvation, for Paul himself expressed relief that in his mission to Corinth he himself 'did not baptize any...except Crispus and Gaius' (1 Cor. 1:14)."[4]

*The Holman Illustrated Bible Dictionary* provides this insight: "The Bible clearly teaches that salvation is appropriated solely by faith based on the grace of God. Baptism, being an act of man, can never cleanse a person of sin or procure God's forgiveness (Rom. 4:3)."[5]

*The MacArthur Bible Commentary* states: "...It does not teach that baptism saves, since the lost are condemned for unbelief, not for not being baptized."[6]

*Matthew Henry's Commentary* tells us "that nothing else but unbelief shall damn men."[7]

And in *Systematic Theology*, Wayne Grudem summarizes: "Therefore, we must conclude that no *work* is necessary for salvation. And therefore *baptism* is not necessary for salvation...to say that baptism or any other action is *necessary* for salvation is to say that we are not justified by faith alone, but by faith plus a certain 'work,' the work of baptism."[8]

The fourth verse that mentions baptism is Acts 19:4, which states, "John verily baptized with the baptism of repentance." This verse is not saying that water baptism is necessary for salvation. The context is this: "...These men knew only about John's baptism.... They did not know that Christ had died....He (Paul) reminded them that when John baptized with the baptism of repentance, he urged them to believe…on Christ Jesus."[9] So this verse cannot be used as a proof text of baptism as a requirement for salvation.

In addition, the thief on the cross was saved, and obviously he had not been baptized. The Bible states that God is no respecter of persons (Acts 10:34; Rom. 2:11; Eph. 6:9; Col. 3:25). What He did for the thief was no exception. Also, if baptism were a requirement, then if someone was about to die in a plane crash, or in an automobile accident, or in a foxhole, then God would be incapable of saving those very people who would be crying out for Him. God's arm would therefore be short to save, and we know that cannot be the case. To prove that, look at these verses:

> » John 6:40: "This is the will of him that sent me, that every one which seeth the Son, and believeth on him, may have everlasting life: and I will raise him up at the last day."
>
> » Romans 10:13: "For whosoever shall call upon the name of the Lord shall be saved."
>
> » 1 Timothy 2:4: "…who will have all men to be saved."
>
> » 1 Timothy 2:6: "[Christ Jesus] gave himself a ransom for all."
>
> » Hebrews 2:9: "He by the grace of God should taste death for every man."
>
> » 1 John 2:2: "…but also for the sins of the whole world."

As you can see, it is God's will for all to be saved, and all who call upon Him *will* be saved. If water baptism were a requirement for salvation, then "all" couldn't call upon Him, and these verses would not be true. Baptism is a wonderful benefit and certainly it is a blessing—and every Christian should obey the Word of God and experience it. But please don't add to the clear teaching of salvation by faith alone. Ephesians 2:8–9 declares: "For by grace are ye saved through faith; and that not of yourselves: it is the gift of God: not of works, lest any man should boast."

Titus 3:5 also tells us: "Not by works of righteousness which we have done, but according to his mercy he saved us, by the washing of regeneration, and renewing of the Holy Ghost."

Finally, Billy Graham states: "Only one answer will give a person the certain privilege, the joy of entering heaven. 'Because I have believed in Jesus Christ and accepted Him as my Savior.'"[10]

# APPENDIX A

## Scriptures of Prophecy About Jesus and Their Fulfillment

- » He would be the seed of a woman (Gen. 3:15; Gal. 4:4).

- » He is the promised seed of Abraham (Gen. 18:18; Acts 3:25).

- » He is the promised seed of Isaac (Gen. 17:19; Matt. 1:2).

- » He will descend from the tribe of Judah (Gen. 49:10; Luke 3:33).

- » He is the promised seed of Jacob (Num. 24:17; Luke 3:34).

- » He is the heir to the throne of David (Isa. 9:7; Matt. 1:1).

- » His place of birth is prophesied (Micah 5:2; Matt. 2:1).

- » His time of birth is prophesied (Dan. 9:25; Luke 2:1–2).

- » He is born of a virgin (Isa. 7:14; Matt. 1:18).

- » A massacre of infants takes place at His birth (Jer. 31:15; Matt. 2:16).

» The holy family is forced to flee into Egypt (Hosea 11:1; Matt. 2:14).

» He has a ministry in Galilee (Isa. 9:1–2; Matt. 4:12–16).

» He is a prophet (Deut. 18:15; John 6:14).

» He is a priest, like Melchizedek (Ps. 110:4; Heb. 6:20).

» He is rejected by the Jews (Isa. 53:5; John 1:11).

» Some of His characteristics are listed in these verses (Isa. 11:2; Luke 2:52).

» His triumphal entry into Jerusalem is prophesied (Zech. 9:9; John 12:13–14).

» He is betrayed by a friend (Ps. 41:9; Mark 14:10).

» He is sold for thirty pieces of silver (Zech. 11:12; Matt. 26:15).

» The money is returned and used for a potter's field (Zech. 11:13; Matt. 27:6–7).

» Judas's office is to be taken by another (Ps. 109:7–8; Acts 1:16–20).

» False witnesses accuse Him (Ps. 27:12; Matt. 26:60–61).

» He is silent when accused (Isa. 53:7; Matt. 26:62–63).

» He is smitten and spat upon (Isa. 50:6; Mark 14:65).

» He is hated without a cause (Ps. 69:4; John 15:23–25).

» He suffers violently and vicariously (Isa. 53:4–5; Matt. 8:16–17).

» He is crucified with sinners (Isa. 53:12; Matt. 27:38).

» His hands and feet are pierced (Ps. 22:16; John 20:27).

» He is mocked and insulted (Ps. 22:6–8; Matt. 27:39–40).

» He is given gall and vinegar (Ps. 69:21; John 19:29).

» He hears prophetic words repeated in mockery (Ps. 22:8; Matt. 27:43).

» He prays for His enemies (Ps. 109:4; Luke 23:34).

» His side is pierced (Zech. 12:10; John 19:34).

» Soldiers cast lots for His coat (Ps. 22:18; Mark 15:24).

» Not a bone of His is broken (Ps. 34:20; John 19:33).

» He is buried with the rich (Isa. 53:9; Matt. 27:57–60).

» He is resurrected from the dead (Ps. 16:10; Matt. 28:9).

» He ascends into heaven (Ps. 68:18; Luke 24:50–51).

Jesus Himself read the passage in Isaiah that stated, "The Spirit of the Lord GOD is upon me; because the LORD hath anointed me to preach good tidings unto the meek; he hath sent me to bind up the brokenhearted, to proclaim liberty to the captives, and the opening of the prison to them that are bound; to proclaim the acceptable year of the LORD..." (Isa. 61:1–2). He told them that "this day is this scripture fulfilled in your ears" (Luke 4:21). He announced that He was the fulfillment of all the prophecies about the coming Messiah. He also said this in Luke 24:27, where it states, "And beginning at Moses and all the prophets, he expounded unto them in all the scriptures the things concerning himself." Jesus is the eternal Son of God.

# APPENDIX B

## Comments on Authenticity of the Scriptures

Dr. Gleason L. Archer, BD, from Princeton and Ph.D., from Harvard Graduate School, received training in Latin, Greek, French, and German at Harvard University. He majored in Hebrew, Aramaic, and Arabic...Akkadian and Syriac, teaching courses on these subjects....He obtained a full law degree....He personally inspected most of the important archeological sites....This background enabled Dr. Archer to become an expert in the issue of alleged errors and contradictions in Scripture: "In my opinion this charge can be refuted and its falsity exposed by an objective study done in a consistent, evangelical perspective....I candidly believe I have been confronted with just about all the biblical difficulties under discussion in theological circles today—especially those pertaining to the interpretation and defense of Scripture....As I have dealt with one apparent discrepancy after another and have studied the alleged contradictions between the biblical record and the evidence of linguistics, archeology, or science, my confidence in the trustworthiness of Scripture has been repeatedly verified and strengthened by the discovery that almost every problem in Scripture that has been discovered by man, from ancient times until now, has been dealt with in a completely satisfactory manner by biblical text itself—or else by objective archeological information."

Given the fact that Dr. Archer has graduated from Princeton and Harvard, has done extensive studies in archeology and other areas, has become fluent in fifteen languages, and has received full training in legal evidences, the above statement can hardly be summarily dismissed by critics.[1]

Dr. Robert Dick Wilson (Ph.D., Princeton), an Old Testament authority and author of *A Scientific Investigation of the Old Testament*, could read the New Testament in nine different languages by the age of twenty-five. In addition, he could repeat from memory a Hebrew translation of the entire New Testament without missing a single syllable, and do the same with large portions of the Old Testament. He proceeded to learn forty-five languages and dialects and was also a master of paleography and philology: "I have made it an invariable habit never to accept an objection to a statement of the Old Testament without subjecting it to a most thorough investigation, linguistically and factually."...His conclusion was that no critic has ever succeeded in proving an error in the Old Testament.[2]

Dr. John Warwick Montgomery graduated from Cornell University with distinction in philosophy, Phi Beta Kappa. Then he went on to earn a Ph.D. from the University of Chicago, a second doctorate in theology from the University of Strasborg, France, and seven additional graduate degrees in theology, law, library science, and other fields. He has written over 125 scholarly journal articles, plus forty books, many of them defending the Christian faith against skeptical views.[3]

Rev. John W. Haley examined 900 alleged problems in Scripture, concluding, "I cannot but avow, as the [conclusion]…every difficulty and discrepancy in the Scripture is…capable of a fair and reasonable conclusion."[4]

Dr. William Arndt…in his own study of alleged contradictions and errors in the Bible, [said,] "We may say with full conviction that no instances of this sort occur anywhere in the Scriptures."[5]

Dr. Craig L. Blomberg (PhD, University of Aberdeen), associate professor of New Testament, Denver Seminary, and author of *The Historical Reliability of the Gospels*…[says,] "Virtually all the so-called contradictions in the Gospels can be readily harmonized."[6]

Dr. John Warwick Montgomery says: "To be skeptical of the resultant text of the New Testament books is to allow all of classical antiquity to slip into obscurity, for no documents of the ancient period are as well attested bibliographically as the New Testament."[7]

The distinguished archaeologist, Professor Albright…[had this to say:] "The Table of Nations" [in Genesis 10], according to Albright, "remains an astonishingly accurate document."[8]

## In Regard to the Empty Tomb

N.T. Wright, former professor of New Testament Studies at Oxford University in England, explains, "The historian has to say, 'How do we explain the fact that this movement spread like wildfire with Jesus as the Messiah, even though Jesus had been crucified?'" The answer has to be, it can only be because He was raised from the dead.[9]

Harold Mattingly, who was an emeritus professor at the University of Leeds, writes in his history text: "The apostles, St. Peter and St. Paul, sealed their witness with their blood."[10]

Tertullian writes that "no man would be willing to die unless he knew he had the truth."[11]

Harvard law professor Simon Greenleaf [says], "The annals of military warfare afford scarcely an example of the like heroic constancy, patience, and unflinching courage. They had every possible motive to review carefully the grounds of their faith, and the evidence of the great facts and truths which they asserted."[12]

History professor Lynn Gardner rightly asks, "Why would they die for what they knew to be a lie? A person might be deceived and die for a falsehood. But the apostles were in a position to know the facts about Jesus' resurrection and they still died for it."[13]

Tom Anderson, former president of the California Trial Lawyers Association, states, "Let's assume that the written accounts of His appearances to hundreds of people are false. I want to pose a question.

With an event so well publicized, don't you think that it's reasonable that one historian, one eyewitness, one antagonist would record for all time that he had seen Christ's body?...The silence of history is deafening when it comes to the testimony against the resurrection."[14]

Paul L. Maier concludes, "If all the evidence is weighed carefully and fairly, it is indeed justifiable, according to the canons of historical research, to conclude that [Jesus' tomb] was actually empty.... And no shred of evidence has yet been discovered in literary sources, epigraphy, or archaeology that would disprove this statement."[15]

Sir Lionel Luckhoo is considered by many to be the world's most successful attorney after 245 consecutive murder acquittals. This brilliant lawyer rigorously analyzed the historical facts of Christ's resurrection and finally declares, "I say unequivocally that the evidence for the resurrection of Jesus Christ is so overwhelming that it compels acceptance by proof which leaves absolutely no room for doubt."[16]

Professor Thomas Arnold, author of a famous three-volume *History of Rome* and the chair of modern history at Oxford,...says, "I have been used for many years to study the histories of other times, and to examine and weigh the evidence of those who have written about them, and I know of no one fact in the history of mankind which is proved by better and fuller evidence of every sort, to the understanding of a fair inquirer, than the great sign which God has given us that Christ died and rose again from the dead."[17]

British scholar Brooke Foss Westcott, who was a divinity professor at Cambridge University, says: "Taking all the evidence together, it is not too much to say that there is no historic incident better or more variously supported than the resurrection of Christ. Nothing but the antecedent assumption that it must be false could have suggested the idea of deficiency in the proof of it."[18]

William Lane Craig concludes that "when you...[use] the ordinary canons of historical assessment, the best explanation for the facts is that God raised Jesus from the dead."[19]

Simon Greenleaf was one of the greatest legal minds America has produced. He was the famous Royal Professor of Law at Harvard University....While at Harvard, Greenleaf wrote a volume in which he examines the legal value of the apostles' testimony to the resurrection of Christ. He observes that it is impossible that the apostles "could have persisted in affirming the truths they had narrated, had not Jesus actually risen from the dead..." Greenleaf concludes that the resurrection of Christ is one of the best-supported events in history according to the laws of legal evidence administered in the courts of justice.[20]

There are now more than 5,300 known Greek manuscripts of the New Testament. Add over 10,000 Latin Vulgate and at least 9,300 other early versions and we have more than 24,000 manuscript copies of portions of the New Testament in existence. No other document of antiquity even begins to approach such numbers and attestation.[21]

F.F. Bruce…comments, "There is no body of ancient literature in the world which enjoys such a wealth of good textual attestation as the New Testament."[22]

Frederic G. Kenyon…[declares,] "It is reassuring at the end to find that the general result of all these discoveries of the authenticity of the Scriptures [is] our conviction that we have in our hands, in substantial integrity, the veritable Word of God."[23]

# Notes

### CHAPTER 1:
### GONE IN THREE SECONDS!

1. Maurice Rawlings, *Beyond Death's Door* (Nashville, TN: Thomas Nelson, 1978), 98–99. Permission requested.
2. Taken from *Heaven* by Randy Alcorn. Copyright © 2004 by Randy Alcorn. Permission requested of Tyndale House Publishers, Inc. All rights reserved.

### CHAPTER 2:
### WHY SHOULD I GO TO HEAVEN?

1. Billy Graham, *Death and the Life After* (Nashville, TN: Thomas Nelson, 1987). Viewed at Google Books. Permission requested.
2. Alcorn, *Heaven*, 23.
3. Charles Stanley, *Charles Stanley's Handbook for Christian Living* (Nashville, TN: Thomas Nelson, 2001), 271–272. Viewed at Google Books.
4. Billy Graham, *The Heaven Answer Book* (Nashville, TN: Thomas Nelson, 2012), 128. Viewed at Google Books.
5. Thomas Aquinas, *Summa Theologiae*, as quoted in Robert A. Peterson, *Hell on Trial* (Phillipsburg, NJ: Presbyterian and Reformed Publishing, 1995), 109. Permission requested.
6. Christopher W. Morgan and Robert A. Peterson, eds., *Hell Under Fire* (Grand Rapids, MI: Zondervan, 2004), 210. Permission requested.
7. Chuck Missler, "Heaven: What Happens When You Die?" (Coeur d' Alene, ID: Koinonia House, 2003), audio tape.
8. Peterson, *Hell on Trial*, 68–69.
9. Graham, *Death and the Life After*, 185–186.

### CHAPTER 3:
### WHAT IS TRUTH?

1. William Lane Craig, *Reasonable Faith* (Wheaton, IL: Crossway Books, 2008), 173–174. Permission requested.
2. Ibid., 174–175.
3. Robert Jeffress, *Outrageous Truth* (Colorado Springs, CO: Waterbrook, 2008), 29.

4. Taken from *Lies That Go Unchallenged* by Charles Colson. Copyright © 2005 by Charles Colson. Permission requested of Tyndale House Publishers, Inc. All rights reserved.
5. Taken from *The Origin of the Bible* edited by Philip Wesley Comfort. Copyright © 2003 by Tyndale House Publishers, Inc.. Permission requested of Tyndale House Publishers, Inc. All rights reserved.
6. *The American Heritage Dictionary of the English Language*, 4th edition (Boston: Houghton-Mifflin, 2006), s.v. "judge."
7. Franklin Graham, *The Name* (Nashville, TN: Thomas Nelson, 2002), 58–59.
8. Taken from *How Now Shall We Live* by Charles Colson. Copyright © 1999 by Charles Colson. Permission requested of Tyndale House Publishers, Inc. All rights reserved.
9. MSNBC.com, "Belief in Hell Boosts Economic Growth, Fed Says," July 27, 2004.
10. Ulysses S. Grant, as quoted in *The Evidence Bible*, 791.
11. Goodreads.com, "Flannery O'Conner Quotes," http://www.goodreads.com/quotes/4951-the-truth-does-not-change-according-to-our-ability-to (accessed July 5, 2013).
12. Grant R. Jeffrey, *Creation* (Colorado Springs, CO: Water-Brook Press, 2003), 50. Permission requested.
13. Rod Parsley, *Culturally Incorrect* (Nashville, TN: Thomas Nelson, 2007), 154.
14. Charles Crismier, *Renewing the Soul of America* (Richmond, VA: Elijah Books, 2002), 310, 313–314.
15. Colson, *Lies That Go Unchallenged*, 165.

CHAPTER 4:
INFORMED OR IGNORANT?

1. As quoted in Ted Koppel, "Lulling Viewers Into a State of Complicity," *Nieman Reports*, vol. 54, no. 3, Fall 2000, http://www.nieman.harvard.edu/reports/article/101836/Lulling-Viewers-Into-a-State-of-Complicity.aspx (accessed July 8, 2013).
2. Thomas Edison, as quoted in *The Evidence Bible*, 77.
3. John D. Morris, *The Young Earth* (Green Forest, AR: Master Books, 1994).
4. Lee Strobel, *The Case for Faith* (Grand Rapids, MI: Zondervan, 2000).
5. Jeffrey, *Creation*.

6. Ibid.
7. Ibid.
8. Bert Thompson, "Biblical Accuracy and Circumcision on the 8th Day," ApologeticsPress.org, http://apologeticspress.org/apcontent.aspx?category=13&article=1118 (accessed July 8, 2013).
9. Perry Stone, *Breaking the Jewish Code* (Lake Mary, FL: Charisma House, 2009), 28.
10. Steve A. Austin, "Springs of the Ocean," http://www.icr.org/article/180/ (accessed July 8, 2013).
11. Planetearthwater.com, "What Is Distilled Water?", http://www.planetearthwater.com/distillation.php (accessed July 8, 2013).
12. Jeffrey, *Creation.*
13. *The Evidence Bible*, 1634.
14. Henry Morris, *Defending the Faith* (Green Forest, AR: Master Books, 1999), 130.
15. Jeffrey, *Creation.*
16. Ibid.
17. Ibid.
18. Ibid.
19. Ibid.
20. *The Evidence Bible*, 709.
21. *How to be Born Again*, by Billy Graham, © 1989 Billy Graham, used by permission, all rights reserved.
22. A. W. Tozer, *Jesus, Our Man in Glory* (n.p.: Wingspread Publishers, 2009), 22.
23. Colson, *How Now Shall We Live?*, 379.
24. William Penn, as quoted in *The Evidence Bible*, 721.

CHAPTER 5:
NEAR-DEATH EXPERIENCES

1. Maurice Rawlings, *To Hell and Back* (Nashville, TN: Thomas Nelson, 1993), 20. Permission requested.
2. Maurice Rawlings, *To Hell and Back, NDE Near-Death Experience Documentary*, http://archive.org/details/ToHellAndBackByDoctorRawlingsNdeNearDeathExperienceDocumentary (accessed July 8, 2013).
3. Dale Black, *Flight to Heaven* (Grand Rapids, MI: Bethany House, 2010), 99–105.
4. Ibid., 186.

5. Mickey Robinson, *Falling to Heaven* (Cedar Rapids, IA: Arrow, 2003), 97–100.
6. B. W. Melvin, *A Land Unknown: Hell's Dominion* (Maitland, FL: Xulon Press, 2005).
7. Ibid.
8. Ibid.
9. Ibid.
10. Stone, *Secrets From Beyond the Grave* (Lake Mary, FL: Charisma House, 2010), 54–56.
11. Rawlings, *To Hell and Back*, NDE Near-Death Experience Documentary.
12. Rawlings, *To Hell and Back*.
13. Ibid.
14. Ibid.
15. Ibid.
16. Ibid.
17. Ibid.
18. Ibid.
19. Ibid.
20. Rita Bennett, *To Heaven and Back* (Grand Rapids, MI: Zondervan, 1997), 44–48. Permission requested.
21. Ibid.
22. Jerry Newberry, *My Journey*, pamphlet.

CHAPTER 6:
CLINICAL DEATH EXPERIENCES

1. Thomas Welch, *Oregon's Amazing Miracle* (Portland, OR: Acorn House, 2007). Permission requested.
2. Ibid.
3. Ibid.
4. Gary L. Wood, *A Place Called Heaven* (Mustang, OK: Tate Publishing & Enterprises, LLC, 2008). Permission requested.
5. Ibid.
6. Ibid.
7. Richard Sigmund, *A Place Called Heaven* (Unionville, MO: Cleft of the Rock Ministries, 2004), back cover, interior text. Permission requested.
8. Ibid.
9. Ibid.

10. Don Piper, *90 Minutes in Heaven* (Grand Rapids, MI: Revell, a division of Baker Publishing Group, 2004). Permission requested.
11. Ibid.
12. Rawlings, *Beyond Death's Door*, 74–76, 101.
13. Ibid.
14. Ibid.
15. Richard Eby, *Caught Up Into Paradise* (Grand Rapids, MI: Fleming H. Revell, 1978). Used by permission.
16. Ibid.
17. Kenneth E. Hagin, *I Believe in Visions* (Tulsa, OK: Rhema Bible Church, 1984). Permission requested.
18. Ibid.
19. Ibid.
20. Rawlings, *Beyond Death's Door*, 94–95.
21. Ibid.

## CHAPTER 7:
### DREAMS AND VISIONS OF THE AFTERLIFE

1. Bill Wiese, *Hell* (Lake Mary, FL: Charisma House, 2008), 92–93.
2. Erwin Lutzer, *One Minute After You Die* (Chicago: Moody Publishers, 1997), 25. Reprinted by permission.
3. Norvel Hayes, *Understanding the Ministry of Visions* (Cleveland, TN: Norvel Hayes Ministry, 1992), 13.
4. John Bunyan, *Visions of Heaven and Hell* (New Kensington, PA: Whitaker House, 1998).
5. Ibid.
6. Ibid.
7. Ibid.
8. Stone, *Secrets From Beyond the Grave*, 121–123.
9. Lutzer, *One Minute After You Die*, 80–81.
10. Lori Haider, *Saved From Hell* (N.p: Lori Haider Ministries, n.d.). Permission requested.
11. Ibid.
12. Ibid.
13. Ibid.
14. Ibid.
15. Ibid.
16. Ibid.
17. Ibid.

18. Rebecca Springer, *Within Heaven's Gates* (New Kensington, PA: Whitaker House, 1984), 10, 12.
19. Ibid., 44
20. Stone, *Secrets From Beyond the Grave*, 90–91.
21. Pearl Ballew Jenkins, *My Vision of Heaven and Hell* (Murphy, NC: n.p., 1984), 7–9.
22. Ibid.
23. Ibid.
24. Eby, *Caught Up Into Paradise*, 228–230.
25. Hagin, *I Believe in Visions*, 44–45.
26. Ibid.

## CHAPTER 8:
### DO YOU BELIEVE IN AN AFTERLIFE?

1. Lutzer, *One Minute After You Die*, 31.
2. Stone, *Secrets From Beyond the Grave*, 25, 129.
3. Graham, *Death and the Life After*, 187–189.
4. Graham, *The Heaven Answer Book*, 3, 73.
5. Alcorn, *Heaven*, 24.
6. Wayne Grudem, *Systematic Theology* (Grand Rapids, MI: Zondervan, 1994), 1140.
7. Walter Martin, *The Kingdom of the Cults* (Grand Rapids, MI: Bethany House Publishers, a division of Baker Publishing Group, 2003), 127. Permission requested.
8. John Eldredge, *The Journey of Desire: Searching for the Life We've Only Dreamed Of* (Nashville, TN: Thomas Nelson, 2000).
9. Alcorn, *Heaven*, 311–312.
10. Ibid., 91, 241.
11. Lutzer, *One Minute After You Die*, 82–84.
12. Stone, *Secrets From Beyond the Grave*, 179.
13. Edward Donnelly, *Heaven and Hell* (Great Britain: Bell & Bain, Ltd., 2001), 65–66.
14. *The Evidence Bible*, 1216.
15. Stone, *Secrets From Beyond the Grave*, 41.

## CHAPTER 9:
### GOD DOESN'T GIVE UP

1. Graham, *Death and the Life After*, 190.

2. Charles H. Spurgeon, *The Soul Winner* (New York: Cosimo, Inc., 2007), 89.
3. William MacDonald, *Believer's Bible Commentary* (Nashville, TN: Thomas Nelson, 1995), 1060.
4. John MacArthur, *The MacArthur Bible Commentary* (Nashville, TN: Thomas Nelson, 2005), 898.
5. Matthew Henry, *Matthew Henry's Commentary on the Whole Bible* (Peabody, MA: Hendrickson Publishers, 2005), 1344.
6. Merrill F. Unger, *Unger's Commentary on the Old Testament* (Chicago: Moody Press, 1981), 1498.

## CHAPTER 10:
## THE "DEAD" COULD TELL US A THING OR TWO!

1. MacDonald, *Believer's Bible Commentary*.
2. *Vine's Expository Dictionary*, 286, 300.
3. Henry, *Matthew Henry's Commentary*, 432.
4. David W. Baker, T. Desmond Alexander, and Bruce K. Waltke, *Obadiah, Jonah, Micah: Tyndale Old Testament Commentaries* (Downers Grove, IL: InterVarsity Press, 1988), 114, 116; Leslie C. Allen, *The Books of Joel, Obadiah, Jonah, and Micah: New International Commentary on the Old Testament* (Grand Rapids, MI: Wm. B. Eerdmans Publishing Co., 1976), 216–217.

## CHAPTER 11:
## WHAT RELIGIONS TELL US

1. Stone, *Secrets From Beyond the Grave*, 181.
2. Ibid., 39.
3. Graham, *How to be Born Again*.
4. Ibid., 182. Permission requested.
5. John Ankerberg and John Weldon, *Facts on Life After Death* (N.p.: The John Ankerberg Show, 2011). Used by permission.
6. Martin, *The Kingdom of the Cults*.
7. Ibid.
8. Fritz Ridenour, *So What's the Difference?* (Ventura, CA: Gospel Light/Regal Books, 1967, 1979, 2001). Used by permission.
9. Ibid.
10. Alcorn, *Heaven*, 347.

11. Ridenour, *So What's the Difference?*, 102, 104–105.
12. Martin, *The Kingdom of the Cults*, 301, 303.
13. Josh McDowell, *The Best of Josh McDowell: A Ready Defense* (Nashville, TN: Thomas Nelson, 1993), 273–275, compiled by Bill Wilson. Permission requested.
14. Rawlings, *To Hell and Back*, 100.
15. Martin, *The Kingdom of the Cults*, 150–156.
16. Ibid.
17. Ibid.
18. McDowell, *The Best of Josh McDowell: A Ready Defense*, 332–334.
19. Ibid., 341–342, 344, 346.
20. Ed Decker, *Mormonism: What You Need to Know* (Eugene, OR: Harvest House, 1997), 1.
21. Stone, *Secrets From Beyond the Grave*, 181.

## CHAPTER 12:
### WHY IS CHRISTIANITY UNIQUE?

1. Henry Morris and Martin E. Clark, *The Bible Has the Answer* (Green Forest, AR: Master Books, 1976), 146.
2. Craig, *Reasonable Faith*, 361.
3. Chuck Missler, *Prophecy 20/20* (Nashville, TN: Thomas Nelson, 2006).
4. McDowell, *The Best of Josh McDowell: A Ready Defense*, 27–28.
5. Ibid., 31.
6. As quoted in John Ankerberg and John Weldon, *Knowing the Truth About the Reliability of the Bible* (Eugene, OR: Harvest House, 1998), 24. Permission requested.
7. As quoted in Josh McDowell, *Evidence That Demands a Verdict* (Nashville, TN: Nelson Reference, 1999).
8. Ibid.
9. Ibid.
10. *The Evidence Bible*, 1357; McDowell, *Evidence That Demands a Verdict*.
11. Edward K. Rowell and *Leadership* editors, *1001 Quotes* (Grand Rapids, MI: Baker Books, 2008), 57.
12. Arthur Blessitt, *The Cross* (Colorado Springs, CO: Authentic Books: 2008), 73.
13. *The Evidence Bible*, 301.

14. Gregory Dickow, *The Power to Change Today* (New York: Faith Words, 2009).

## CHAPTER 13:
### WHAT DOES THE BIBLE SAY ABOUT HELL?

1. MacDonald, *Believer's Bible Commentary*, 1433.
2. MacArthur, *The MacArthur Bible Commentary*, 1313.
3. Martin, *The Kingdom of the Cults*, 127–128.
4. Robert G. Gromacki, *The New Testament Survey* (Grand Rapids, MI: Baker Book House, 1974), 125.
5. Morgan and Peterson, *Hell Under Fire*, 139.
6. As quoted in Christopher W. Morgan and Robert A. Peterson, eds., *Is Hell for Real or Does Everyone Go to Heaven?* (Grand Rapids, MI: Zondervan, 2011).
7. Morgan and Peterson, *Hell Under Fire*, 167.
8. Alcorn, *Heaven*, 28.
9. Peterson, *Hell on Trial*, 187.
10. Grudem, *Systematic Theology*, 1146.
11. Martin, *The Kingdom of the Cults*, 127.
12. Morgan and Peterson, *Hell Under Fire*, 216.
13. Missler, "Heaven: What Happens When You Die?"
14. Ibid.
15. Donnelly, *Heaven and Hell*, 56.
16. As quoted in Peterson, *Hell on Trial*, 108–109.
17. Ibid., 107.
18. As quoted in Morgan and Peterson, *Hell under Fire*, 227.
19. John Calvin, *Commentary on Matthew, Mark, Luke*, vol. 3, viewed online at Christian Classics Ethereal Library, http://www.ccel.org/ccel/calvin/calcom33.pdf (accessed July 12, 2013).
20. Jonathan Edwards, *Works of Jonathan Edwards*, vol. 2, viewed online at Christian Classics Ethereal Library, http://www.ccel.org/ccel/edwards/works2.xi.ii.html (accessed July 12, 2013).
21. Grudem, *Systematic Theology*, 1146–1147.
22. Lutzer, *One Minute After You Die*, 31–32.
23. Henry, *Matthew Henry's Commentary*, 1746.
24. Robert Jamieson, A. R. Fausset, and David Brown, *Commentary on the Whole Bible* (Grand Rapids, MI: Zondervan, 1961), 919.

25. Grant R. Jeffrey, *Journey Into Eternity* (Minneapolis, MN: Waterbrook Press, 2000), 219.
26. As quoted in Peterson, *Hell on Trial*, 111.
27. Martin, *The Kingdom of the Cults*, 131, 583.
28. Morgan and Peterson, *Hell Under Fire*, 137, 142–144.
29. Ibid., 183.
30. A. W. Pink, *Eternal Punishment* (n.p.: nd.), para. 10, 14, as quoted in Wiese, *Hell*, 274.
31. C. H. Spurgeon, "A Private Enquiry," sermon no 2184, October 9, 1890, and published for reading January 18, 1891, The Spurgeon Archive, http://spurgeon.org/sermons/2184 .htm (accessed July 12, 2013).
32. As quoted in Peterson, *Hell on Trial*, 99.
33. Jack Van Impe, *Beyond the Grave*, VHS/DVD. No further information available.
34. John Wesley, *The Essential Works of John Wesley* (Uhrichsville, OH: Barbour, 2011), 758–762.
35. Theo Wolmarans, *How to Recognize the Voice of God* (Bonaero, South Africa: Theo and Beverly Christian Enterprises, 2009), 68.

## CHAPTER 14:
### HAVE YOU INVESTED IN HEAVEN?

1. David Shibley, *Living as if Heaven Matters* (Lake Mary, FL: Charisma House, 2007), 46.
2. Jentezen Franklin, *Believe That You Can* (Lake Mary, FL: Charisma House, 2008), 138.
3. Charles H. Spurgeon, *The Soul Winner* (New Kensington, PA: Whitaker House, 1995), 9.
4. Rawlings, *Beyond Death's Door*, 112.
5. Graham, *Death and the Life After*, 17.
6. Rowell, *1001 Quotes, Illustrations, and Humorous Stories*, 237.
7. Graham, *Death and the Life After*, 234–235.
8. Shibley, *Living as if Heaven Matters*, 49.
9. Spurgeon, *The Soul Winner*, 184.
10. Ibid., 190.

## CHAPTER 15:
### LOSING LIFE TO FIND IT!

1. MacDonald, *Believer's Bible Commentary*, 1242.
2. Parsley, *Culturally Incorrect*, 162.
3. Ibid.
4. John Bevere, *The Fear of the Lord* (Lake Mary, FL: Charisma House, 2006), 67.
5. Glen Berteau, *Christianity Lite* (Lake Mary, FL: Charisma House, 2013), 4.
6. Bevere, *The Fear of the Lord*, 78.

## CHAPTER 16:
### IS IT REALLY MY OWN WORDS?

1. R. T. Kendall, *Controlling the Tongue* (Lake Mary, FL: Charisma House, 2007), 2.
2. Blessitt, *The Cross*, 215.

## CHAPTER 17:
### BAPTISM—IS IT A REQUIREMENT?

1. MacDonald, *Believer's Bible Commentary*, 1364.
2. Earl Radmacher, Ronald B. Allen, and H. Wayne House, eds., *Nelson's New Illustrated Bible Commentary* (Nashville, TN: Thomas Nelson, 1999), 1243.
3. MacDonald, *Believer's Bible Commentary*, 1365.
4. Lawrence O. Richards, *The Encyclopedia of Bible Words* (Grand Rapids, MI: Zondervan, 1991), 102.
5. Chad Brand, Charles Darper, and Archie England, eds., *Holman Illustrated Bible Dictionary* (Nashville, TN: Holman Bible Publishers, 2003), 168.
6. MacArthur, *The MacArthur Bible Commentary*, 1262.
7. Henry, *Matthew Henry's Commentary*, 1818.
8. Grudem, *Systematic Theology*, 973, 981.
9. MacDonald, *Believer's Bible Commentary*, 1643.
10. Graham, *Death and the Life After*, 186.

## APPENDIX B:
### COMMENTS ON THE AUTHENTICITY OF THE SCRIPTURES

1. Ankerberg and Weldon, *Knowing the Truth About the Reliability of the Bible*, 25.
2. Ibid., 25–26.

3. Ibid., 24.
4. Ibid., 26.
5. Ibid.
6. Ibid., 30.
7. McDowell, *Evidence That Demands a Verdict*, 19.
8. Ibid., 32.
9. Taken from *More Than a Carpenter* by Josh McDowell. Copyright © 2004 by Josh McDowell. Permission requested of Tyndale House Publishers, Inc. All rights reserved.
10. Ibid., 67.
11. Ibid.
12. Ibid.
13. Ibid.
14. Ibid., 68.
15. Ibid., 88.
16. Ibid., 94.
17. Ibid., 93.
18. Ibid.
19. Ibid.
20. Ibid., 94.
21. McDowell, *Evidence That Demands a Verdict*, 39.
22. Ibid.
23. Ibid.

# For Further Information:

Soul Choice Ministries
PO Box 26588
Santa Ana, CA 92799

www.23minutesinhell.com
www.soulchoiceministries.com